Anthony Young

MIGHTY MOPARS 1960-1974

Motorbooks International
Publishers & Wholesalers Inc
Osceola, Wisconsin 54020, USA

© Anthony Young, 1984
ISBN: 0-87938-124-8
Library of Congress Number: 83-19441

Printed and bound in the United States of America.
Book and cover design by William F. Kosfeld.
Cover illustration by Robert Straub.

Motorbooks International is a certified trademark,
registered with the United States Patent Office.

2 3 4 5 6 7 8 9 10

Motorbooks International books are also available at
discounts in bulk quantity for industrial or sales-
promotional use. For details write to Marketing Manager,
Motorbooks International, P.O. Box 2, Osceola,
Wisconsin 54020.

Library of Congress Cataloging in Publication Data

Young, Anthony
  Mighty Mopars, 1960-1974.

  Includes index.
  1. Chrysler automobile—History. 2. Dodge automobile
—History. 3. Plymouth automobile—History.
I. Title.
TL215.C55Y68   1984   629.2'222   83-19441
ISBN 0-87938-124-8 (pbk.)

ACKNOWLEDGMENTS

To Steve Collison, Jeremy Young and Beverly Rae Kimes, editors who had faith in me and gave me my start.

Thanks to Dick Maxwell and Larry Shepard at Chrysler for giving me the personal story behind Dodge and Plymouth performance cars, and for proofing the manuscript. I would especially like to thank Bernard "Moon" Mullins, long-time director of Chrysler Public Relations, for opening the Chrysler photo archives to me. Without this permission, I could not have illustrated the book. Finally, I would like to thank Madryn Johnson of the archives for showing me where I could find what I needed and for allowing me to take any and all photos and brochures.

I have tried to ensure accuracy in this book. In most instances, technical data was compiled from Chrysler brochures and the Direct Connection bulletins. No doubt, there were some cases where Chrysler changed specifications after the brochures were printed. Often, these changes were made to reflect on-going product improvement during the model year. Sometimes new options were added after new model introduction and were thus not in the brochure for that year. The original list prices given in this book are from *Charlton's 1975 Used Car Prices,* covering the years 1968 to 1974. Prices for cars prior to 1968 came from published road tests.

INTRODUCTION

It is interesting to analyze the causes that brought about one of the most exciting eras in automotive styling and performance in America. The sixties were a period of tremendous growth, accomplishment, optimism and self-expression. The automobile was literally a vehicle that embodied all these things, and manufacturers, infused with the same enthusiasm, rose to the task. Gas was cheap, government regulations were minimal and many forms of organized competition gave manufacturers excellent opportunities to go racing. Much of the attention of car manufacturers was focused on the highly visible youth market, and the bulk of their advertising in automotive magazines was aimed at this segment.

The divisions of Chrysler Corporation, although tagged the "number three automaker," were every bit as clever and aggressive as GM and Ford in garnering their share of the performance market during the sixties and early seventies. Mopars were among the most-coveted performance cars on the street. (MoPar was a contraction of Motor Parts, a former division of Chrysler. The word became synonymous with Chrysler automotive products, and eventually MoPar became Mopar.)

Just how did Dodge and Plymouth, with seemingly fewer resources, achieve this enviable position? The answer lies within Chrysler Corporation. The engineers, designers and product planners produced an excellent automobile. With supreme and justifiable belief in their cars, they banged the drum loudly, and every kid from Woodward Avenue to Hollywood Boulevard listened to the beat.

Bernard "Moon" Mullins has been involved with Dodge public relations for more than twenty years. He explained Dodge's involvement with the emerging youth market: "In the early sixties, Dodge had the problem of an older owner group. They needed a younger owner group, and racing was the means by which they decided to get the younger buyer. Racing was a way to promote to the younger people what the older people had already known—that Dodge was an excellent automobile and it was a good strong car that would last a long time. We simply took what was there and made it very well known. We looked upon racing as a promotional activity. What's the point in going racing if you're not going to sell cars?"

Dick Maxwell, long involved with performance cars at Chrysler, was there during the dawn of the performance era. He echoed Mullins' sentiments: "We were virtually invisible on the street—the drive-in scene or the stoplights—wherever you wanted to go. There weren't any of our cars. So, the company got involved in drag racing in 1961, legitimately in 1962, to build an image. The only thing we had on the street in those early days was the 383, which wasn't bad, but it wasn't recognized because in order to go fast, you had to have a Chevy or Ford."

Drag racing by Chrysler actually had its roots in the late fifties. Dick Maxwell was among a small number of Chrysler Institute graduates that decided to form the Ramchargers in the summer of 1958. The purpose of the group was to pool and organize their interest in hot rodding. By early the following year, the Ramchargers had conceived and built a car to compete in C/Altered. Said Maxwell, "The first car we ran was a '50 Plymouth coupe with a 354-ci Hemi, called the *High and Mighty,* at the 1959 Detroit Nationals. That's where the whole thing started. We ran that car in '59 and '60, and finally destroyed the engine and didn't have any parts to repair it. At that time, Jim Thornton was head of the group, and he went to Frank Wylie and sold him on the fact that we should go Super Stock racing."

In 1960, Chrysler introduced the 413 with the wild longhorn, cross-ram manifold. "In 1961," Maxwell continued, "the Ramchargers built a Dodge Dart [This was before the Dart was downsized to a compact] using a shortened version of that manifold, and went Super Stock racing. In '62, we built a 413 Super Stock engine in two versions: 410 hp and 420 hp, which were derived from the production 413, but they used different cylinder heads and a one-piece, cross-ram plenum-type manifold. The street-version longhorn, cross-ram 413 made a whole lot of torque but not much horsepower. The plenum-type manifold didn't make much torque, but it did make a whole lot of horsepower.

"We went out there with our 413's and used them as our image cars on the drag strips and did *very* well with them. That was our first real racing venture—those 413's we built in 1962. And the guys took them out on the street and did even *better.* This stirred up interest in the 383. As a result, we sold a lot of 383's, but not too many 413's because the 413's were really more than most guys could handle. The thing was pretty close to a race car in those days, and it was a real handful on the street. Those things—in '62, '63 and '64, until we brought the 426 Hemi out—were absolutely unstoppable on the street."

Drag racing achieved what Chrysler executives had hoped. With the high-visibility Ramchargers dominating Super Stock racing as touted in the enthusiast magazines, and only slightly detuned versions available off the showroom floors, the stage was set for the most exciting period in the company's performance history.

Follow us back to those thrilling days of . . . The Mighty Mopars.

Anthony Young
Winter 1984

TABLE OF CONTENTS

CHAPTER ONE

Mighty Mopar Muscle— The Engines

*T*he history of Mopar performance is really the history of Chrysler's engines. Chrysler designed and built V-8 engines during the sixties that rivaled anything built by GM or Ford. From the high-winding 273-ci V-8 to the ground-shaking 440 Six-Pack V-8, Chrysler offered the enthusiast a wide selection that had all the bases covered.

The history of the small-block high-performance V-8 began in 1964. That was the year Chrysler introduced the 273-ci V-8 with a bore and stroke of 3.63x3.31 inches. This was the first Chrysler V-8 to benefit from lightweight casting techniques. Referred to as the LA engine, the 273 two-barrel V-8 produced 180 hp. Performance picked up in 1965 with the release of a four-barrel version producing 235 hp at 5200 rpm with 280 pounds-feet of torque at 4000 rpm. Domed pistons replaced the flat-top pistons used in the standard 273, increasing compression to 10.0:1. A high-performance camshaft provided eight degrees more intake and exhaust duration, and an additional twenty-six degrees of overlap. Intake valve lift was increased from 0.395 inch to 0.425 inch. The four-barrel carburetor had primary barrels of 1 7/16-inch diameter and secondary barrels were 1 9/16 inches. In 1966, a limited production version of the 273, rated at 275 hp, was introduced with steel tubing headers, 700-cfm Holley carburetor and a 0.500-inch-lift mechanical camshaft. The 273 V-8 was manufactured through 1969.

The 318-ci V-8 was really the predecessor of the LA engine family. Its bore and stroke was 3.91x3.31 inches. The 318 began production in 1957 and employed established casting techniques which made it a rather heavy block for its displacement. The 318 was never really conceived or built for high-performance applications. It was more a bread-and-butter V-8 with a two-barrel carburetor rated at 230 hp, designed to get good fuel economy. A four-barrel version of this old-style 318 (later engines used lightweight casting techniques) was rated at 260 hp. In 1957, there was a dual four-barrel package that had 290 hp, which was the highest output for the old-style 318.

In 1967, the new LA version of the 318 was introduced. This engine was sixty pounds lighter. The cylinder heads were redesigned, having a wedge configuration similar to the 440 V-8 also offered that year. Yet, horsepower was the same at 230 hp with a compression ratio of 9.2:1. Few parts from the new LA engine were interchangeable with the old 318 A engine. Even by 1970, the 318 remained in a mild state-of-tune. Compression was 8.8:1 to run smoothly on regular gas. Camshaft timing was 240/248 with twenty degrees overlap. Horsepower was 230 at 4400 rpm with 320 pounds-feet of torque at 2400 rpm. It wasn't until 1978 that the new 318 was built with a four-barrel carburetor and manifold borrowed from the 360 V-8. This was the first four-barrel 318 in seventeen years. The 318 V-8 was the only Chrysler passenger-car V-8 engine to survive into the eighties, and thus has the distinction of being manufactured longer and in greater quantities than any other LA engine.

In 1968, Chrysler introduced the 340-ci V-8. Unlike the 318, the 340 was designed as a performance engine. Its bore and stroke was 4.04x3.31 inches. (Note: The 273, 318 and 340 all had the same 3.31-inch stroke.) The heart of the 340 was its big-port, high-flow cylinder heads which measured 2.20 square inches. A well-designed 180-degree, two-level intake manifold aided breathing. In 1968, the four-barrel 340 with a 10.5:1 compression ratio developed 275 hp at 5000 rpm. Torque was 340 pounds-feet at 3200 rpm. Cam timing was 268 degrees intake, 276 degrees exhaust, with forty-four degrees of overlap for cars equipped with automatic transmissions. Cam timing for manual transmission cars was 276/284/52. Intake valve diameter was 2.02 inches, exhaust valve diameter was 1.60 inches. The crankshaft was forged and shot-peened. A special Carter ThermoQuad carburetor had 1⅜-inch primaries and huge 2¼-inch secondaries.

In 1970, the 340 reached its highest state of development as the six-barrel 340 T/A engine. This screamer was used exclusively in the production Plymouth AAR 'Cuda and Dodge Challenger T/A. The engine block was specially cast with thicker webs and pan rails to accommodate four-

The 235-hp four-barrel 273 V-8 was one of the earliest high-performance small-block engines offered by Chrysler.

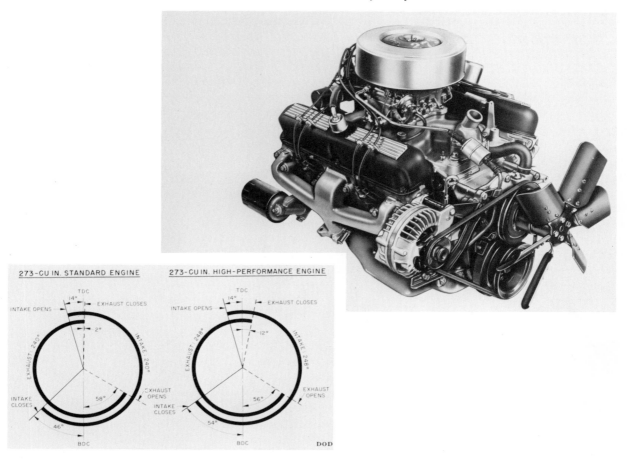

7

bolt main caps. Crankshaft and connecting rods were forged, as in the high-performance four-barrel 340. Pushrods were relocated. The camshaft was radical, with 0.430-inch lift for intake, and 0.445-inch lift for exhaust. The heart of the engine, of course, was the induction system. Three two-barrel Holley carbs sat atop an Edelbrock aluminum intake manifold. The production six-barrel 340 was conservatively rated at 290 hp at 5000 rpm, with 345 pounds-feet of torque at 3400 rpm. Racing versions, with a single four-barrel, destroked to 305 ci, produced an honest 450 hp. The production six-barrel 340 was built for only one year.

In 1972, the 340 lost its 10.5:1 compression ratio in favor of an 8.5:1 compression ratio for emissions reasons. That year, the 340 also picked up the 360 V-8 cylinder heads with smaller intake valves. The 240-hp rating at 4800 rpm reflected the drop in compression and adoption of SAE (Society of Automotive Engineers) net horsepower ratings. Nevertheless, it was still a good, high-performance engine.

Although production of the 340 stopped at the end of the 1973 model year, it continues to be a supremely popular street, strip and racetrack powerplant. Many aftermarket manufacturers, including Chrysler itself, still supply high-performance parts for the 340.

In 1971, Chrysler introduced the 360-ci two-barrel V-8. It differed from the 340 in both bore and stroke. Bore was 4.00 inches and stroke was 3.58 inches. The 360 also differed by having the main web area beefed up to accept a larger main bearing diameter for the cast iron crank. Despite its two-barrel carburetor and a compression ratio of only 8.70:1, it was a reasonably good performer, developing 255 hp at 4000 rpm with 360 pounds-feet of torque at 2400 rpm. In 1972, net horsepower was only 175. The following year, the engine lost five more horsepower, and those bound for California lost yet another seven ponies, due to stricter emission standards.

Help finally arrived in 1974. Besides the two-barrel engine, there were now two 360 V-8's with four-barrel carburetors. One developed 200 hp at 4000 rpm with 290 pounds-feet of torque at 3200 rpm. The other engine developed 245 hp at 4800 rpm with 320 pounds-feet of torque at 3600 rpm. Both four-barrel engines ran with an 8.4:1 compression ratio. Performance deteriorated quickly after that, but the 360 remained in production until the end of the 1980 model run.

The 318 V-8 has never been a high-performance engine, but it has been around a long time.

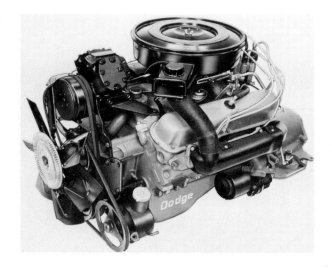

To the rabid street enthusiast, the phrase "there's no substitute for cubic inches" rang true. Big-blocks were really where it was at during the sixties and early seventies. These big-block Chrysler engines were identified as having either a B-block or an RB-block. B-blocks were classified as low-block for their stroke of 3.38 inches. The RB-blocks (for raised-B-block) had a common stroke of 3.75 inches. Displacement varied according to bore.

The 383 V-8 was synonymous with Mopar performance. While there were slightly smaller performance big-blocks offered by Chrysler, most notably the 361-ci V-8, the 383 was the prime mover in millions of Dodges and Plymouths. The 383 was first introduced as a raised-block wedge design in 1959. It had a bore of 4.03 inches. With dual four-barrel carburetion, it produced 345 hp at 5000 rpm and 420 pounds-feet of torque at 3600 rpm.

The following year, 1960, Chrysler introduced the 383 with wild, cast aluminum ram induction. Again, it came with two four-barrel carburetors, but they were suspended over the sides of the engine and fed into a plenum beneath each carburetor with two siamesed runners crossing over the valve covers to the cylinder head on the opposite side of the engine. There were long and short ram manifolds manufactured, but only the long units were offered on passenger cars. The short ram manifold was rare and available only through Mopar parts departments.

Actually, the long and short ram manifolds were identical dimensionally, but they differed internally. In the long ram manifold, the wall between the pair of passages reached all the way from the plenum chamber beneath the carburetor to the cylinder head surface. On the short manifold, this wall extended only 10½ inches from the cylinder head surface. The long version tuned at a lower rpm than the short unit. In other words, the long ram was designed for the street and the short ram for the strip. The short ram manifold also helped Dodge and Plymouth in stock car racing. Plymouth won eight races and Dodge one race on the Grand National circuit in 1960.

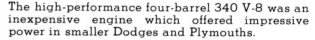

The high-performance four-barrel 340 V-8 was an inexpensive engine which offered impressive power in smaller Dodges and Plymouths.

A 383 with long ram manifolds produced 330 hp at 4800 rpm and 460 pounds-feet of torque at 2800 rpm. With short ram manifolds, it produced 340 hp at 5000 rpm and 440 pounds-feet of torque at 2800 rpm. This hot induction system on the 383 was also offered in 1961, but was dropped at the end of that model year.

In 1960, the factory altered the 383's bore and stroke to 4.25x3.38 inches, making it a low-block. According to Chrysler, the hottest 383 that year came with the famous 300J cylinder heads and a dual four-barrel in-line carburetor setup that produced 343 hp at 5000 rpm. This rare engine was one of the most powerful 383's ever built. A more practical two-barrel 383 with a 10.0:1 compression ratio had 305 hp at 4600 rpm and 410 pounds-feet of torque at 2400 rpm.

There were three high-performance 383's to choose from in 1963. First was a single four-barrel unit with 10.0:1 compression that developed 330 hp at 4600 rpm. Torque was 425 pounds-feet at 2800 rpm. The next most powerful 383 had a slightly higher compression ratio of 10.10:1. With a four-barrel carburetor, it developed 360 hp at 4800 rpm and 470 pounds-feet of torque at 3200 rpm. The top-of-the-line 383 was the dual four-barrel version with compression lowered to 9.60:1. Nevertheless, it produced 390 hp at 4800 rpm and 485 pounds-feet of torque at 3600 rpm. The 305-hp two-barrel 383 was also available for more mundane chores. This year was the apex of 383 engine development, as research and development shifted to the larger-displacement engines.

The 383, however, continued to be a perennial favorite as a performance powerplant for the next eight years. Power output for the 383 was diminished in 1964 so as not to embarrass the horsepower ratings of the larger engines. That year the four-barrel 383 with 10.0:1 compression

The high-performance four-barrel 383 was standard equipment in many Dodge and Plymouth muscle cars.

was rated at 330 hp at 4600 rpm and 425 pounds-feet of torque at 2800 rpm. This engine was the only four-barrel 383 that year. The dual four-barrel 383 was no longer available, but the two-barrel version continued. The horsepower and torque ratings were the same for 1965. In 1966, performance dropped a bit: The four-barrel V-8 was rated at 325 hp at 4800 rpm with 425 pounds-feet of torque at 2800 rpm with a 10.0:1 compression ratio. This remained unchanged for 1967, but Chrysler had not become complacent.

In 1968, the 383 got a shot in the arm. While the two-barrel V-8 was downgraded powerwise, the four-barrel V-8 held its own or was upgraded in performance. The Super Commando 383 developed 330 hp at 5000 rpm and 425 pounds-feet of torque at 3200 rpm. Compression ratio was 10.0:1. The air cleaner was unsilenced and the engine used a dual exhaust. The most powerful 383 that year was a special engine developed exclusively for the low-cost Plymouth Road Runner and Dodge's equivalent, the Coronet Super Bee. Chrysler bumped the output of this 383 by bolting on the high-performance parts designed for the 440 V-8 used in the Plymouth GTX and Dodge Coronet R/T, introduced in 1967.

These high-performance parts consisted of redesigned cylinder heads having larger-diameter exhaust valves (from 1.60 to 1.74 inches), and recontoured ports. Heavy-duty valve springs and rocker arms were employed. The camshaft from the high-performance 440 was also used. Atop the engine sat a Carter AVS four-barrel carburetor and a new, dual-plane intake manifold. The air cleaner was unsilenced and the engine, naturally, used dual exhaust. The rating for this 383 was deliberately conservative; 335 hp at 5200 rpm with 425 pounds-feet of torque at 3400 rpm. In totally stock trim, the engine was capable of launching the Road Runner or Coronet Super Bee through the quarter-mile timing lights at nearly 100 mph with an elapsed time of between fourteen and fifteen seconds. Specifications for this engine remained unchanged for 1969.

In 1970, all three 383's had lowered compression ratios. The two-barrel V-8 was now at 8.7:1, but it still put out 290 hp at 4400 rpm, as it had the previous two years. This engine could now run on regular fuel. The two high-performance four-barrel versions had compression ratios of 9.5:1. Their horsepower and torque ratings remained the same, however, as did their premium fuel requirements. In addition, the 335-hp 383 was switched to a Holley four-barrel carburetor.

In 1971, the high-performance 383 was detuned. Both the two-barrel and four-barrel 383's that year had their compression ratios lowered to 8.5:1 to run on regular fuel. The two-barrel V-8 was rated at 275 hp at 4400 rpm with 375 pounds-feet of torque at 2800 rpm. The four-barrel 383 had 300 hp at 4800 rpm with 410 pounds-feet of torque at 3400 rpm.

This was the last year of 383 production. Over three million 383's had been built by the end of 1971. Thus, Mopar hot rodders looking for a cheap and plentiful engine to bring back to life could do no better than the venerable 383.

In 1972, the 383 was replaced by the 400-ci V-8. The higher displacement was achieved by increasing the bore to 4.34 inches. The 400 V-8 was essentially a smog motor, having a compression ratio of 8.2:1.

There were two 400 V-8's offered by both Dodge and Plymouth in 1972. The two-barrel V-8 had a net horsepower rating of 190 at 4400 rpm, and 310 pounds-feet of torque at 2400 rpm. The four-barrel 400 developed 255 hp at 4800 rpm with 340 pounds-feet of torque at 3200 rpm. Engines equipped with the California Emissions Package had nine fewer horsepower and five pounds-feet less torque. The four-barrel 400's that were equipped with the TorqueFlight automatic transmission were built with cast cranks rather than the forged cranks used in the four-speed manual transmission cars.

The number of 400 versions in 1973 increased to five, but not all were available in the performance B-body Mopars. The first two-barrel 400 developed 175 hp at 3600 rpm and 305 pounds-feet of torque at 2400 rpm. Right behind it was another two-barrel 400 with ten more horsepower and five more pounds-feet of torque. There were three four-barrel 400's. These were rated at 220 hp at 4000 rpm with 310 pounds-feet of torque at 3200 rpm; 245 hp at 4800 rpm with 325 pounds-feet of torque at 3200; and 260 hp at 4800 rpm with 335 pounds-feet of torque at 3600 rpm. These and all subsequent engines reflected the industry-wide practice of using SAE net horsepower and torque readings adopted the previous year. Before, gross readings were taken at the engine's flywheel without accessories; now readings were taken with the engine installed in the car.

By 1974, the 400 V-8 was really starting to feel the effects of tightening emissions controls. Available 400's dropped to three, and neither the two-barrel nor four-barrel V-8's were offered in California. The two-barrel V-8 was rated at 185 hp at 4000 rpm with 315 pounds-feet of torque at 2400 rpm. The two four-barrel engines were rated at 205 and 240 hp. This was the last year you could order a four-barrel 400 with true dual exhaust.

The 413-ci V-8 was one of Chrysler's most formidable performance engines. It would be appropriate to call the 413 a Super Stock engine because it was designed for use in, according to Chrysler literature, "acceleration trials"—meaning drag racing. Plymouth, in fact, called its engine the Super Stock 413. Dodge called its engine the Ram-Charger 413.

The longhorn cross-ram 383 was one of the most exotic and powerful production V-8's of the early sixties.

The 413 was introduced first in Chryslers in 1959, then in Dodges and Plymouths in 1961. It used a raised-block design having a bore and stroke of 4.18x3.75 inches. In single four-barrel trim, it produced 350 hp at 4600 rpm and 470 pounds-feet of torque at 2800 rpm. That year the 413 was also available with long ram manifolds for dual four-barrel carburetors. This engine produced 375 hp at 5000 rpm and 465 pounds-feet of torque at 2800 rpm. While these two engines could be classified as high-performance street engines, Chrysler was at work designing a 413 that was meant for the quarter-mile and oval tracks.

In 1962, the Max Wedge 413 was released. Its name signified the maximum level of performance development of that displacement having wedge-shaped combustion chambers. The intake and exhaust ports were twenty-five percent larger than the previous year, improving engine breathing at high rpm. The heat crossover passage to the intake manifold was eliminated to ensure that a denser fuel/air charge reached the cylinders. Cylinder head gaskets were stainless steel for extra durability. Exhaust valve diameter increased a whopping quarter inch to 1.88 inches. Intake valve diameter remained the same at 2.08 inches. The camshaft had 0.510-inch lift with 300 degrees duration. The lifters were mechanical (solid). To prevent valve float above 6000 rpm, Chrysler used dual valve springs with a combined pressure of 340 pounds at full lift. Instead of stamped steel rocker arms, cast nodular parts were used to withstand the stress.

The cast aluminum manifold was of a new ram-induction design to provide increased power above 4000 rpm. It had a series of passages fifteen inches long, fed by two staggered 650-cfm Carter AFB four-barrel carburetors. This one-piece manifold nestled between the valve covers and made servicing much easier compared to the long ram manifold of 1961.

In 1972, the 400-ci V-8 replaced the 383. It was available in both two-barrel and four-barrel versions. This engine had an 8.2:1 compression ratio, improved drivability and reduced emissions.

Chrysler turned to TRW to supply the special pistons. The Max Wedge 413 was available with 11.0:1 or 13.5:1 pistons. The latter could not be run on pump-grade 100 octane gas, but had to use aviation fuel!

The connecting rods were up to the task. These rods were forged, which was standard practice by 1962, but also magnafluxed to check for any hairline cracks.

Chrysler engineers had done extensive testing to come up with free-flowing exhaust manifolds that would be durable for strip, oval track or serious street racing. What they concocted, essentially, were cast iron headers. These manifolds swept up and back; this was done because there wasn't enough room below the engine to allow four individual runners coming off each cylinder head, since this would interfere with the chassis.

The exhaust system was designed with racing in mind. Bolted to the exhaust manifolds were three-inch head pipes which fed directly to exhaust cutouts that could be removed for racing. Just ahead of the cutouts, the 2½-inch street exhaust pipes picked up and fed back into two large reverse-flow aluminized mufflers from the Chrysler New Yorker. The exhaust system was finished off with two-inch tail pipes.

Chrysler engineers made sure no detail of the 413's performance was overlooked. As an example, all belt pulleys were deep-grooved for better belt retention at high speed. Even the oil pan was scrutinized, using baffles to prevent the crankshaft from frothing the oil and ensuring proper lubrication under hard acceleration.

Mated to the 413 was a standard heavy-duty three-speed manual transmission with floor shifter. A heavy-duty TorqueFlight automatic transmission was optional.

The 413 Max Wedge proved to be a formidable strip performer. The National Hot Rod Association (NHRA) record books for 1962 show four class records established by Dodges powered by the Ram-Charger 413 alone. In SS/S class, Dick Landy clocked a quarter-mile elapsed time of 12.71 seconds. Bill "Maverick" Golden, racing in SS/SA, stopped the timing lights in 12.50 seconds. The *Golden Lancer,* running in A/FX, set a 12.26-second quarter-mile time. Jim Nelson, racing in the wild AA/D class, set an astounding 8.59-second record. With strip tires and proper rear end gears, mid-twelve-second times were commonplace.

At the Fremont, California, Drag Strip on July 15, 1962, Tom Grove, driving the *Melrose Missle,* became the first racer to crack the twelve-second barrier in a production stock passenger car with factory option engine. Behind the wheel of the Plymouth with the 413 Super Stock engine, Grove clocked an 11.93-second elapsed time at 118.57 mph.

Tom Grove had this to say about his 413's performance: "I feel the Plymouth has the strongest potential in the Super Stock field—more horsepower, and less car weight per cubic inch than any of the competition. The engine is a beauty—none better. And Plymouth is just starting to really tap its power. I have pulled numerous 430 rear-wheel horsepower readings on Melrose's 500-horse dyno. These are steady readings that have been held—not flash readings. The best that the 1962 *Missle* has pulled is a steady 450 rear-wheel horsepower. Can any of your slide-rule mathematicians compute the actual shaft horsepower? Wow!"

With the introduction of the 426 Max Wedge in 1963, the 413 Max Wedge was dropped from the Dodge and Plymouth lines, but the 413 in milder states-of-tune remained available in Chrysler cars. For 1963, you could order a single four-barrel 413 developing 340 hp at 4600 rpm and 470 pounds-feet of torque at 2800 rpm. Compression ratio was 10.0:1. There was also a dual four-barrel setup that developed 390 hp at 4800 rpm and 485 pounds-feet of torque at 3600 rpm.

There were three 413's to choose from in 1964. The single four-barrel unit had the same specs as the year before, except for a slightly higher compression ratio of 10.10:1. There was also another four-barrel 413 with 360 hp at 4800 rpm and 470 pounds-feet of torque at 3200 rpm. The dual four-barrel 413 suffered a drop in compression to 9.6:1, but it still pumped out 390 hp and had a higher torque rating than even the 426 Max Wedge.

The dual four-barrel 413 was dropped in 1965, leaving two 413's with single four-barrel carburetion. Horsepower and torque readings were the same as the year before, but Chrysler fiddled with the compression ratio again, returning to 10.0:1. This was the last year of the 413's production.

The 413 was really Chrysler Corporation's first drag racing engine, putting Dodge and Plymouth on the performance map and capturing the attention and interest of all enthusiasts. This engine has a special place in the hearts and minds of Chrysler engineers and executives as well as Mopar fans.

The 426, also with a wedge cylinder head design, first appeared in 1962, installed only in top-of-the-line Chryslers. It was not available in Dodges or Plymouths. This engine was not a high-performance power-plant in the drag racing sense. But this changed in 1963, when Chrysler introduced the 426 Max Wedge Stage II engine. The primary difference between this engine and the 413 Max Wedge, of course, was the larger bore of 4.25 inches, resulting in 426 ci.

The magnificent Max Wedge 413 of 1962 was intended for sanctioned drag racing, but was raced on the street as well. The Max Wedge 426, identical in appearance, superseded it in 1963.

The 426 Max Wedge was strictly designed for racing, and was offered in Plymouths as the Super Stock 426 and in Dodges as the 426 Ramcharger (the spelling was changed). Aside from the displacement, the visual differences between the 426 and 413 Max Wedge engines were slight. A Plymouth brochure showed its Super Stock 426 with a black, seven-blade fan. A Dodge brochure showed its 426 Ramcharger with a chrome, four-blade fan. In every other respect, the two were identical.

Like the 413 Max Wedge, the 426 Max Wedge was available with a choice of two compression ratios. The 11.0:1 engine developed 415 hp at 5600 rpm with 470 pounds-feet of torque at 4400 rpm. The 13.5:1 engine developed 425 hp at 5600 rpm and 480 pounds-feet of torque at 4400 rpm. Based on these figures, the 426 Max Wedge developed only five more horsepower and five pounds-feet more torque than the 413 Max Wedge. The elapsed times and trap speeds of Mopars running the 426 Max Wedge were no better than those for the 413 Max Wedge. Tom Grove, racing for Melrose Motors in Oakland, California, switched from the 413 to the 426 Max Wedge, but did not improve his times by doing so.

In 1964, Chrysler introduced the 426 Max Wedge Stage III. Improvements included larger-capacity Carter carburetors and larger air cleaners to accommodate them; a new camshaft with 320 degrees of overlap; modified combustion chambers with deeper clearance notches around the valves; 13.0:1 pistons replaced by 12.5:1 pistons in the higher-compression engine; and new exhaust manifolds designed for NASCAR racing with tuned, equal-length twenty-one-inch passages, which dumped into two large steel tubes and then funneled into a 3½-inch-diameter head pipe on each side. Chrysler referred to this exhaust manifold system as Tri-Y headers.

With the introduction of the 426 race Hemi in 1964, racers had an even more powerful engine to use. The Hemi was designed to surpass the 426 Max Wedge, but the Hemi's production was limited, so the 426 Max Wedge remained a viable and affordable alternative. The 426 Max Wedge stayed in production through 1964.

There also was a street version of the 426 in 1964, but it lacked virtually all the Max Wedge components—with good reason. While you could walk into any Dodge or Plymouth dealer and order your Mopar with a 426 Max Wedge, the trouble started when you took delivery and tried to drive it home. The engine was almost undrivable on the street; the 426 Max

The 1964 426 street wedge V-8 with four-barrel carburetion was the biggest high-performance engine you could order that year.

Wedge was a racing engine, pure and simple. The 426 street wedge, while lacking the power of its snarling brother, also had none of the headaches.

The 426 street wedge had one four-barrel carburetor mounted on a cast iron intake manifold, and had provision for crossover heat to the manifold to aid warmup. The exhaust manifolds were conventional—not the wildly shaped units used on the Max Wedge. Compression was a healthy 10.3:1. Horsepower was 365 at 4800 rpm with 470 pounds-feet of torque at 3200 rpm.

The last year for the 365-hp 426 street wedge was 1965. Mopar fans who dreamed of having a 426 street Hemi derived from the 426 race Hemi would not have to dream much longer.

Legendary is a word often bandied about when it comes to cars. If any engine earned this label, it was the 426 Hemi.

On February 23, 1964, three Hemi-powered Plymouths and a Hemi-powered Dodge swept the Daytona 500, 1-2-3-4. It was a stunning victory which set the world of NASCAR racing on its ear. News of this awesome engine spread like wildfire.

As most Mopar enthusiasts know, the 426 Hemi was not the first Chrysler Hemi, but it was the best. Whereas the Hemis of the fifties were passenger-car engines, the 426 Hemi of 1964 was conceived strictly as a race engine, from the oil pan up. Its purpose was to win big on the NASCAR circuit and dominate organized drag racing.

Chrysler met the letter of the law in the NASCAR rule book with regard to the minimum production run of engines. However, the 426 Hemi was too successful for its own good. It was making a mockery of the competition, and NASCAR put its foot down. Instead of building several hundred blue-printed Hemis a year, Chrysler had to build several thousand and offer them in production vehicles. Chrysler had invested too much time and money developing the Hemi to walk away from NASCAR permanently (although it did so for one year); the company turned a liability into an asset and detuned the Hemi for the street.

This photo clearly shows the equal-length cast iron exhaust manifolds with Tri-Y headers on this Dodge 426 Ramcharger race engine of 1964. Plymouth called its version the Super Stock 426.

The street Hemi was introduced in 1966 in the Plymouth Belvedere and Dodge Coronet and Charger. When you compare the specifications of the 1964, 1965 and 1966 track and drag engines with the 1966 street engine, it's startling how similar they are. Only modifications to make it drivable on the street were made. The street and race Hemi had the same cast iron, stress-relieved block with a bore and stroke of 4.25x3.75 inches. The forged, shot-peened and Nitride-hardened crankshaft was the same for both street and race Hemi, as well as the impact-extruded pistons, cross-bolt main bearing caps, forged connecting rods, iron cylinder heads and mechanical lifters.

The biggest differences between the street and race Hemi were the intake and exhaust manifolds. The intake manifold on the circle-track Hemi in 1964 and 1965 was a conventional aluminum dual-plane, single four-barrel manifold. The track Hemi of 1966 used an aluminum plenum-ram single four-barrel manifold. For drag racing, the 1964 Hemi used an aluminum dual four-barrel plenum-ram manifold. The 1965 drag Hemi used the same manifold, but it was cast in magnesium; and to reduce weight even further, it used aluminum cylinder heads. The exhaust manifolds on the race Hemi were naturally of the header type, using 2¼-inch-outside-diameter tubing with steel castings or plates bolted to the cylinder heads. Length varied from thirty to forty inches.

The street Hemi had necessarily milder valve train specifications. The camshaft had both intake and exhaust durations of 276 degrees, compared to the 1966 track Hemi's 328 degrees. Valve overlap was fifty-two degrees on the street engine and 112 degrees on the track engine. Intake and exhaust valve lifts were 0.48 inch and 0.46 inch, respectively, while the track Hemi had 0.565-inch lift for both intake and exhaust. The valve springs were softer on the street Hemi to reduce camshaft wear. Racing valves were used in the street Hemi with an intake valve diameter of 2.25 inches and exhaust valve diameter of 1.94 inches.

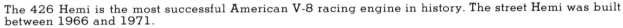

The 426 Hemi is the most successful American V-8 racing engine in history. The street Hemi was built between 1966 and 1971.

The street Hemi's compression ratio was lowered from 12.5:1 used for the racing Hemi to 10.25:1, using pistons with lower domes.

The intake manifold on the street Hemi was an aluminum dual-plane design with two Carter four-barrel carburetors mounted in tandem. Because the racing cylinder heads had no provision for intake manifold heat, a pair of tubes running off the right exhaust manifold to the intake manifold was needed to make the cold-blooded Hemi streetable.

A massive, chromed air cleaner straddled both carburetors, instead of the individual air cleaners used in the past.

Did someone ask about horsepower? The 1966 street Hemi was conservatively rated at 425 hp at 5000 rpm, with 490 pounds-feet of torque at 4000 rpm. The street Hemi was an expensive option, costing over a thousand bills in 1966 dollars. It was attractive to those who had to have the ultimate in performance and image on the street, who more than likely took it to the drags on the weekends.

Because the Hemi was so highly developed, the street version was improved in only two significant ways during its production from 1966 through 1971: In 1968, the duration of the solid lifter camshaft was bumped from 276 to 284 degrees. The overlap was also increased, from fifty-two to sixty degrees. In 1970, Chrysler switched from solid to hydraulic lifters, which required less frequent tuneups. The advertised horsepower and torque ratings were not changed, however.

Designed for racing, the 426 Hemi was a record setter wherever cars were raced. During the sixties, Bill and Bob Summers were avid racers and Mopar supporters. Known as The Summers Brothers, they embraced the Hemi as the ultimate racing engine, even in stock trim. In 1965, they set new World Unlimited Class and International Class A speed records with their thirty-two-foot-long, streamlined *Goldenrod,* powered by four fuel-injected Chrysler Hemis. On the Bonneville Salt Flats, the 2,400-hp vehicle hit 409.695 mph for the Flying Kilometer and 409.277 for the Flying Mile. The following year, The Summers Brothers returned to Bonneville with a Hemi-powered Plymouth Satellite and set an American B/Production stock car record of 156.35 mph.

Despite the fact that Chrysler was absent from the stock car ovals in 1965 due to a dispute with NASCAR's Bill France over the 426 Hemi's production status, records were still being set at Daytona. On February 26, 1965, Lee Roy Yarbrough set a new closed-course record of 181.88 mph with a fuel-injected and blown Hemi-powered Dodge Coronet.

NASCAR's most successful racer, Richard Petty, didn't sit idle with his Plymouth on the sidelines in 1965. He had a 1965 Barracuda specially fitted with a 426 Hemi before he hit the drag strip circuit, and won B/Altered class that year.

An even wilder vehicle seen on the quarter mile was not a car, but a pickup truck. *The Little Red Wagon* was one of the most popular drag racing rigs at strips around the country. The brainchild of Dick Branstner, Roger Lindamood, Jim Schaeffer and John Collier, *The Little Red Wagon* was a Dodge A-100 compact pickup dropped onto a custom, heavy-duty chassis with a mid-engine fuel-injected 426 Hemi for power. Wheelstands were the rage at drag strips during the sixties, and *The Little Red Wagon* performed them effortlessly while setting ten-second elapsed times at 130 mph.

All across America, the 426 Hemi not only became the engine to beat, but the engine to race. Professionals and amateurs agreed it was the most powerful and successful racing engine ever built. To list the races the 426 Hemi has won would be an impossible task.

That is a distinction that the 426 Hemi holds to this day. Chrysler stopped building the Hemi at the end of 1971, but aluminum Hemi blocks and cylinder heads manufactured by Keith Black and Milodon continue to supply an insatiable market for this most famous of Chrysler engines.

The Chrysler 440-ci V-8 wedge engine was the largest ever bolted into a Dodge or Plymouth. The corporation introduced the 440 in 1966. It had a bore and stroke of 4.32x3.75 inches. This engine, with a four-barrel carburetor and 10.10:1 compression ratio, was not considered a high-performance engine like the 426 street Hemi introduced that year. There were two 440 V-8's in 1966. One developed 350 hp at 4400 rpm with 480 pounds-feet of torque at 3200 rpm, and the other engine developed 365 hp at 4600 rpm with 480 pounds-feet of torque at 3200 rpm. These engines were designed to power the largest and heaviest Chryslers, Dodges and Plymouths. Chrysler engineers saw the performance prospects in the 440 for the growing high-performance street scene, and got to work.

In 1967, Chrysler introduced the Super Commando 440 in a brand new performance car—the Belvedere GTX. This same engine, called the 440 Magnum, powered Dodge's new performance car, the Coronet R/T. The ad for the GTX touted the engine's displacement status: "Supercar. And how! The standard GTX powerplant just happens to be the biggest GT engine in the world!"

The Super Commando 440 and 440 Magnum were meant to fill in Dodge's and Plymouth's performance engine lineup, fitting in between the 383 and the 426 Hemi. The 440 started life as a bored 426 street wedge. This was a rugged block and used forged crankshaft and connecting rods, but Chrysler engineers saw no need for forged pistons. Most of the development work for the high-performance 440 went into the engine's induction system.

The first thing the engineers tackled was the cylinder heads. These heads had ten percent larger ports than those in the 1966 engine. The intake and exhaust ports were redesigned to smooth the flow of the fuel and air mixture into the cylinders and spent gases out of the cylinders. The in-

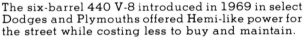

The six-barrel 440 V-8 introduced in 1969 in select Dodges and Plymouths offered Hemi-like power for the street while costing less to buy and maintain.

take valve diameter stayed the same at 2.08 inches, but the exhaust valve diameter increased from 1.60 inches to 1.74 inches. The intake manifold was redesigned to match the increase in the cylinder head ports. Chrysler chose a Carter AVS four-barrel carburetor to deliver the fuel. Atop the carburetor sat a dual-snorkel unsilenced air cleaner.

This engine also received a high-performance camshaft to complement the induction system. The rather mild camshaft in the '66 440 was nixed for a hotter one with 268-degrees intake duration, 286-degrees exhaust duration, fifty-four-degrees overlap, 0.450-inch intake lift, and 0.465-inch exhaust lift.

The exhaust manifolds were unique to this engine in 1967. These heavy-duty cast iron units had smoother passages than those on the 1966 engine, although they weren't as convoluted as those on the 426 Max Wedge or the 426 Hemi.

The undercar exhaust system was patterned closely after that used on the 426 Hemi. The exhaust manifolds emptied into 2½-inch pipes which fed into two reverse-flow mufflers, ahead of which was a crossover pipe to aid torque and reduce exhaust "rap." Tail pipes were 2¼ inches in diameter.

This engine was rated at 375 hp at 4600 rpm with a stump-pulling 480 pounds-feet of torque at 3200 rpm. Compression ratio was 10.10:1. The 350-hp 440 remained, but the 365-hp 440 was dropped in 1967.

In 1968, the 440 received redesigned cylinder heads having larger combustion chambers for better emissions. The pistons were also redesigned, extending farther into the combustion chamber to maintain the compression ratio.

During the 1969 model year, Chrysler released the most significant performance engine since the 426 Hemi. That engine was the 440 Six-Pack. The clever name was coined by long-time Chrysler executive Moon Mullins, and Phil Ingledrum. Six-Pack referred to the triple two-barrel induction system. Choosing to go with this system was really a smart marketing move. Chrysler had explored single four-barrel and dual four-barrel carburetor systems, but had never used a triple two-barrel setup on its B-block. Enthusiasts had always thought such an induction system to be the ultimate on the street, and it was used successfully on Pontiac's GTO and Chevrolet's Corvette. The 440 Six-Pack was the obvious next step to take with the 440.

The rugged and smooth TorqueFlight automatic transmission was mated to the most powerful engines Chrysler built. It underwent continuous improvement during the sixties.

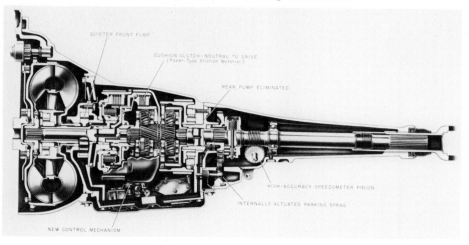

The foremost features of this engine were the three Holley two-barrel carburetors that sat atop a custom Edelbrock aluminum intake manifold, with a combined flow capacity of over 1,200 cfm, nearly double that of the four-barrel 440. While cruising down the street or highway, the engine was fed by the center carburetor having 1½-inch barrels. Under hard acceleration, the front and rear carburetors with 1¾-inch barrels would kick in. The 440 Six-Pack had an open air cleaner spanning all three carburetors.

In producing horsepower, the 440 Six-Pack compared favorably with the 426 Hemi. The 440 Six-Pack developed 390 hp at 4700 rpm with 490 pounds-feet of torque at 3200 rpm; the 426 Hemi didn't develop that amount of torque until 4000 rpm. Street and strip races between a 440 Six-Pack and 426 Hemi were sometimes close.

In 1970, the compression ratio on the four-barrel 440 was dropped to 9.7:1, but was still rated at 375 hp. The compression ratio for the 440 Six-Pack remained at 10.5:1.

In 1971, both four-barrel and six-barrel 440's dropped slightly in compression. The four-barrel V-8 dropped to 9.5:1 and had 370 hp at 4600 rpm with 480 pounds-feet of torque at 3200 rpm. The 440 Six-Pack was rated at 385 hp at 4700 rpm with 490 pounds-feet of torque at 3600 rpm. Its compression ratio was 10.3:1. This was the last year for the 440 Six-Pack.

For 1972, Chrysler adopted SAE net horsepower ratings and lowered compression ratios on all engines. The 440 Six-Pack was scheduled for 1972 production, but at the last minute Chrysler decided to drop it. The four-barrel 440 became increasingly rare, and wasn't even available in the Dodge Charger or Plymouth Barracuda.

Horsepower continued to plummet with each passing year. The 440 was eventually phased out of passenger cars in the late seventies.

CHAPTER TWO

Mopar Performance Roots 1960-1964

Chrysler started out the first year of the sixties with a bang. Dodge introduced a new model, the Dart. Both two- and four-door models had a 118-inch wheelbase, four inches shorter than the full-size Dodges. The Dart lineup included the low-priced Seneca, the mid-priced Pioneer and the top-of-the-line Phoenix.

Underneath its unibody construction, the Dart rode on torsion bar front suspension with semi-elliptic rear springs. Handling for Darts with the smaller engines was acceptable, but the bigger engines taxed the Dart's aplomb. The standard drum brakes weren't up to the task of slowing down the more muscular Darts either, but special police brakes with larger and wider drums could be ordered.

The Dart was offered with a 225-ci slant six, or one of three V-8's. The V-8 displacements were 318, 361 and 383 ci. Performance fans ordered the D-500 ram-inducted 383.

News spread slowly about the Dart as a performance car, and it wasn't until the restyled 1961 Dart appeared that *Motor Trend* and *Hot Rod* tested it. Base list price for the Dart Phoenix two-door or four-door was $2,796. The D-500 engine option added $312.60.

Despite the four-door's 4,005-pound weight, the Dart with the D-500 engine, TorqueFlight automatic transmission and 3.23:1 Power Lok différential posted the following times: 0-60 mph in 6.8 seconds, 0-80 mph in 11.9 seconds and a quarter-mile time of sixteen seconds at 94 mph.

The three-speed manual column shift was standard, but a Hurst floor shift conversion kit could be ordered if you wanted to improve your times.

"For all-out performance," wrote *Motor Trend,* "the 1961 car buyer has to look no further than Dodge's newest Dart with its optional powerplant, the brutal D-500 ram-induction engine."

Hot Rod magazine decided to hop up the engine and check its top speed capability using over-the-counter Chrysler parts. With short ram manifolds, 284-degree mechanical camshaft and other modifications, the D-500 Dart streaked across the dry El Mirage lake bed at 134.12 mph.

Gas economy wasn't really an issue in 1961, but the D-500-equipped Dart achieved 13.1 mpg at the then-legal 65 mph limit.

Plymouth's equivalent to the Dart in 1960 was the 118-inch-wheelbase Sport Fury. It was available with many of the same power train options as the Dart. The Sport Fury didn't have the same performance image as the Dart, however, and Plymouth sales in general were at their lowest levels in years. Fortunately for both Plymouth and Dodge, the muscle car era was about to dawn.

Plymouth styling during the early sixties was nothing if not eclectic. This was a period when automakers were expected to change the styling of each model every year, and they could afford to do so. The styling of the Sport Fury of 1960 and the Fury of 1961 had no rhyme or reason, but then, it was the end of the fin era and Plymouth stylists were searching for answers.

A more impressive showing was the new Plymouth Valiant of 1960. The car was conceived and designed under strict security. It was aimed at a new market segment, and called "compact." Both two- and four-door versions had a 106.5-inch wheelbase with a curb weight of 2,750 pounds.

Automotive publications thought the Valiant's styling was European inspired. Indeed, it was a handsome car among the crop of 1960 automobiles, and it holds up well even today. Two styling features helped the Valiant stand out. A trim strip below the car's beltline ran from the front wheelwell toward the back, then swept up and around the rear wheel opening and finished at the taillights. This would set a trend among both Plymouth and Dodge cars. Another distinguishing styling feature was the bogus spare tire cap on the trunk, similar to the Imperial. The Valiant chrome script appeared in the center of the tire cap and on the front fenders, and the name appeared again on the front grille.

The virile-looking longhorn cross-ram manifolds of the 383-ci D500 V-8 engine in this 1961 Dodge Dart drew admiring looks.

The Valiant came with the 101-hp 170-ci slant six. Even in 1960, Plymouth saw the performance capabilities in its new compact. It wasn't long before the Valiant hit the racetrack.

"When NASCAR decided to run a compact road race in conjunction with the 1960 Daytona 500," recalled Dick Maxwell, "all the factories got involved. We built a fleet of seven Hyper Pak Valiants with 148-hp 170-ci sixes having a single four-barrel with ram manifold. It was a Plymouth runaway. We finished first through seventh. Our cars were so fast, NASCAR never did that race again."

The Hyper Pak engine was an option on the production Valiant. Compression ratio was increased from 8.5:1 in the stock engine to 10.0:1. It had a rating of 148 hp.

In response to the Valiant, Dodge introduced the Lancer in 1961. The wheelbase and sheetmetal were identical to those of the Valiant, but the Lancer had different front and rear end styling, which many thought more attractive. The Lancer was more luxurious than the Valiant, having a higher price tag. The Lancer 170 two-door sedan sold for $2,312.

The Lancer's base powerplant was the 170 slant six, but a new 225-ci slant six with 145 hp was optional. This engine was also available as a Hyper Pak, and it had an impressive rating of 196 hp. Lancers equipped with the Hyper Pak 225 could do 0-60 mph in 8.6 seconds and the quarter mile in 16.4 seconds. The 225 slant six was later offered with an aluminum block, weighing forty-five pounds less than the iron-block 170 and eighty pounds less than the iron-block 225.

In 1962, the Lancer GT appeared. It was primarily an appearance package. Instead of the front bench seat, there were two handsome bucket seats and other deluxe interior trim. Lancer GT medallions were mounted on the doors inside, below the vent window. List price was $2,562.

Although the bigger Dodges were beginning to appear at drag strips around the country in impressive numbers, the *Golden Lancer* of Dode Martin and Jim Nelson was just about the hottest compact on the strips in 1962. Stuffed into the engine compartment was a 413 Ramcharger V-8. It raced successfully in A/FX class. It could do the quarter mile in 12.68 seconds at 113 mph.

This was the second and last year for the Lancer. Dodge had a new compact coming off the drawing boards to take its place.

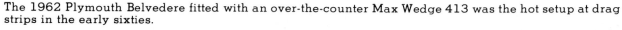
The 1962 Plymouth Belvedere fitted with an over-the-counter Max Wedge 413 was the hot setup at drag strips in the early sixties.

25

Nineteen sixty-two was also the year the mid-size Dodges and Plymouths dropped in size. Wheelbase went from 118 inches to 116 inches. At a time when longer, lower and wider was the trend, this seemed to run counter to buyer wishes. The reduction in size and weight, however, proved a boon to drag racers.

The ultimate street engines to haul you and your mighty Mopar down the quarter mile were the 305-hp four-barrel 361, the 305-hp two-barrel 383 or the 340-hp four-barrel 413. In the spring of 1962, Chrysler released the 410-hp and 420-hp Max Wedge 413's. Most of these Max Wedge 413's were installed in Plymouth Furys and Belvederes, and Dodge 330 and 440 series cars, terrorizing quarter-mile competitors from coast to coast.

In an effort to build showroom traffic and sales, Plymouth loudly touted its restyled 1962 Sport Fury. A brochure issued to dealers read:

The Plymouth Valiant Signet 200 of 1962 had distinctive exterior detailing.

The 1962 Sport Fury shared all sheetmetal with the Belvedere, but had a jazzier interior.

"Sport Fury/for the man who wants to go first class—fast! The luxury leader of the low-priced field—with sizzling performance to make your prospects eyes pop!"

The 1962 Sport Fury had a long list of standard features that made it attractive to buyers. The 305-hp 361 V-8 was the standard powerplant with dual exhaust. The interior sported bucket seats with center console and distinctive interior trim. The car was laden with chrome inside and out. The paint colors were inviting: silhouette black, ermine white, cherry red, pale gray, pale blue, luminous cordovan, luminous blue and luminous brown. The 1962 Sport Fury was really a razzle-dazzle car. Plymouth limited production to give it some exclusivity.

A new Valiant model for 1962 helped to fill the void left by the Lancer GT. That car was the Signet 200. It came with pleated, leatherlike bucket seats, custom-tailored interior trim, deep-pile carpeting, special trunk lid emblem (the bogus tire cap on the trunk lid was now gone), different grille and headlamp frames, distinctive grille emblem and special side moldings. Despite all this, the Signet 200 was America's lowest-priced hardtop with bucket seats.

For 1963, the mid-size Plymouths were completely redesigned. The outrageous styling of the previous year's cars was gone. The 1963 models all showed the same clean, uncluttered, rational lines, and weighed roughly 300 pounds less than before.

Among the mid-size offerings were seven Furys (including the Sport Fury), four Belvederes and three Savoys. All had the same 116-inch wheelbase, 205-inch length (except for station wagons) and seventy-five-inch width. New self-adjusting brakes were the biggest piece of engineering news for 1963. Even more significant was Chrysler's new five-year, 50,000-mile warranty.

As before, the top-of-the-line Plymouth was the Sport Fury. With the 330-hp Golden Commando 383, it could do 0-60 mph in 7.2 seconds, and the quarter mile in 15.9 seconds.

If you were serious about racing your Plymouth, the Max Wedge 426, new for 1963, could be ordered. It was available in 415-hp and 425-hp versions.

Although short-lived, the 1962 Dodge Lancer GT had a handsome interior with leatherlike vinyl bucket seats.

The push-button gear selector for the TorqueFlight automatic transmission is on the left of the 1962 Valiant V-200 instrument panel.

There was some reshuffling in the Dodge camp for 1963. In a combined move, the Lancer was eliminated and the Dart became a redesigned and downsized compact. The new Dart's wheelbase for all models but station wagons was now 111 inches. Since it was now a compact, all V-8's were dropped. The 170-ci and 225-ci six were the only engines. Needless to say, the 1963 Dart was not the choice of drag racers. However, a number of enterprising racers did shoehorn V-8's into the car to take advantage of its 2,850-pound curb weight. One magazine tested a Dart equipped with a 426 Ramcharger engine. This car could do 0-60 mph in 4.2 seconds and the quarter mile in 12.5 seconds. The Dart GT, with its six-cylinder engine, didn't offer much in the way of performance, but it did include spruced-up appointments. Better performance days for the Dart lay ahead.

To counter the ire of the buying public over its 116-inch-wheelbase cars, Dodge increased the wheelbase to 119 inches for 1963. These cars exhibited cleaner lines and less inconsequential ornamentation.

Plymouth introduced the Valiant convertible with either power or manually operated top in 1963.

In 1963 the Dart was downsized to a compact, yet it rode on a 111-inch wheelbase. This Dart GT was one of nine models in the Dart line.

The styling was of less interest to Dodge performance fans than what was under the hood. There were four 383's to choose from. The two-barrel 383 developed 305 hp. There was a 330-hp and 360-hp four-barrel 383, and the dual four-barrel 390-hp 383 was still available. The 340-hp four-barrel 413 was the largest street engine available in a Dodge. For racing, the 426 Ramcharger was offered in 415-hp and 425-hp versions.

To prove it seriously supported drag racers in 1963, Dodge offered front end aluminum sheetmetal to give its cars a weight advantage on the strip. When you ordered your Dodge with the 426 Ramcharger engine, you could also order the aluminum front end package as an option. The package included aluminum front fenders, hood, functional hood scoop, fender wells and other parts. An aluminum front bumper was also included. The aluminum front end package dropped the weight of the Dodge by nearly 150 pounds.

Dodge had made all the right decisions for 1983. The buying public embraced the larger-wheelbase and better-looking cars enthusiastically. And, the factory's high-visibility Ramchargers drag racing team was an excellent promotional effort to convince younger buyers that Dodge made an exciting product. The sales figures said it all: In 1963, Dodge sold over 350,000 cars, a new-car sales record.

It could be said that 1964 truly marked the dawn of the muscle car era. That year, the Pontiac GTO appeared. While other performance cars preceded it—the Chevy Impala SS 409 is an example—the GTO was the first muscle car with an image and specific market buyer in mind. The GTO instantly established itself as *the* car to have on the street or at the drive-in, but not because it was the fastest. The 413 Mopars could run rings around the GTO, but it would be several years before Dodge and Plymouth would sell cars with image to match their outstanding performance.

Once again, Plymouth restyled its 116-inch-wheelbase cars. The most noticeable changes were to the front end and roof. The roof of the two-door coupe had a convertible motif with tapering rear pillars. This higher roof gave one inch more headroom. In the Sport Fury, there was an attractive new center console with a stick-shift-type gear selector for the automatic transmission.

The engine lineup was the same as the year before, plus two new engines. The 365-hp four-barrel 426 high-performance V-8 was new, and offered significant acceleration improvements over the 383 V-8. A Sport Fury powered by this engine could do 0-60 mph in 6.8 seconds and the

The top street performance power train for 1964 Dodges and Plymouths was Chrysler's new A-833 four-speed manual transmission bolted to the 365-hp 426 street wedge.

quarter mile in 15.2 seconds. Also new was the awesome 426 Hemi, available for racing only.

A new Chrysler-engineered, fully synchronized, floor-mounted manual four-speed transmission was available on Commando and 426 Super Stock engines. The three-speed manual-shift transmission was improved. Optional rear axle ratios for V-8's were limited to 2.76 with the TorqueFlight, and 3.23 with the four-speed transmissions.

Building on a worldwide record of sales success in 1963, the Valiant moved into 1964 with design changes giving better economy, reliability and performance. The Valiant was the leading export compact abroad and in Canada, and was cutting a wide swath in United States compact sales.

Changes in the 1964 Valiant included a restyled front end and minor cosmetic changes to the taillights. Most of the other changes that year were mechanical.

Like its bigger brothers, the Valiant had a new optional manual four-speed transmission with Hurst shift linkage. Also new was the Sure-Grip differential; while touted as a safety feature, it was of more interest to Mopar fans from a performance standpoint.

Valiant enthusiasts could put the new manual four-speed transmission and Sure-Grip differential options to good use by ordering the new 273-ci 180-hp V-8, which was a mid-year introduction.

With the availability of the 273-ci V-8 in 1964, the Valiant became the lowest-priced V-8 automobile in the world.

For many years Chrysler has chosen to use torsion bar front suspension. This illustration for the 1961 Dodge Lancer is representative.

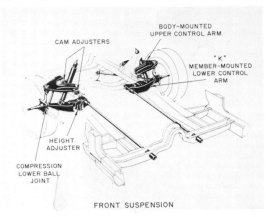

The 1964 Dodge Dart GT compact interior reflected the youthful spirit Dodge was promoting to attract the younger, less-affluent buyer.

There were significant changes to Dodge's offerings in 1964 as well. The 119-inch-wheelbase Dodges had restyled front ends. The outer headlights produced strong, circular forms in the sheetmetal. The new Chrysler Turbine 1963 show car may have influenced the styling of the 1964 Dodge front end. From the windshield back, the styling was the same as the 1963 Dodge, except for different taillights and minor trim.

While the 1964 Dodges were sleepers in the looks department, they were gaining respect on the street and the drag strip. Efforts both inside and outside Chrysler Corporation were doing much to build a formidable performance reputation.

Don Beebe of Automotive Promotions and Jim Nelson and Dode Martin of Dragmasters pooled their talents to build two awesome Dodge race cars. They started with a pair of two-door sedans. The 426 Ramcharger wedge engines were stroked to 480 ci. Each engine received a high-performance crankshaft, aluminum connecting rods and pistons, camshaft, cylinder heads, GMC 6-71 blower with Hilborn injector scoop and magnesium manifold, and headers. The cars were fitted with all the other usual drag racing equipment. These two cars were called the Dodge Chargers—two years before the 1966 Charger would appear. They each developed 800 hp and were billed as the "World's Fastest S/FX Drag Cars." They stirred up tremendous interest in Dodge cars at drag strips across the country.

Dodge's own Ramchargers team was setting records wherever it raced. At the 1964 Winternationals in Pomona, California, the team took Top Stock Eliminator against the fastest cars in the country. Its winning time was 12.44 seconds at 115.08 mph. The team set a new A/FX record of 118.42 mph in 12.03 seconds and took Top Stock Eliminator at the Detroit Dragway NHRA regional. There were similar victories at drag strips in other states. The Ramchargers team was a crowd pleaser wherever it raced, and added credibility to Dodge's production performance cars.

Dodge became really serious about selling its racing machinery in 1964. Cars completely equipped with Dodge's new Maximum Performance Package rolled off the Hamtramck, Michigan, assembly line in the spring of that year. These cars were powered by the new 426-ci Dodge Hemi-Charger acceleration engine, with dual four-barrel carburetors and 12.5:1

The first 1964 Dodge, completely factory equipped with the Maximum Performance Package for drag racing, is readied for shipment. Note the narrow-profile front tires and magnesium wheels.

compression ratio, developing an advertised 425 hp at 6000 rpm. The hood, front fenders and doors were of aluminum, as were various smaller sheet-metal parts. A lightweight front bumper, lightweight bucket seats and magnesium front wheels were also included.

Racers who didn't want this whole package could still opt for the 426 Ramcharger engine, available with either 415 hp or 425 hp, depending on compression ratio. The top street engine to have in your '64 Dodge was the Hi-Performance 426 V-8. With 10.3:1 compression ratio and four-barrel carburetor, it developed 365 hp.

There were two 383 V-8's for 1964. The four-barrel 383 had 330 hp; the two-barrel 383 had 305 hp.

To get the power to the pavement, there was a new floor-mounted four-speed manual transmission. This was the same as used in Plymouths. It was optional with the 383 V-8's and the 426 Ramcharger; it was standard with the 365-hp 426 engine.

The TorqueFlight automatic transmission was popular with drag racers for its durability, and was still controlled through Chrysler's unique push-button gear selector on the dash.

Having been restyled the year before, the 1964 Dart had only minor cosmetic changes. The description of the Dart GT in the 1964 Dodge brochure was contradictory and bewildering, yet typical of the time when America's romance with the automobile was approaching its peak: "Here's high-performance styling with a rakish emphasis—sports-car flavor with 'big car' flair! Dart GT for 1964 is more massive, yet more graceful—more elegant and yet more impressive-looking. ("GT" is for "Gran Turismo"—a car designed for "grand touring." In Dart GT, you travel rapidly in luxury, comfort *and* style!)."

There really wasn't much substance to all this high-blown prose for the Dart GT, but if you were willing to spend some extra money, you could come reasonably close. A new four-speed manual transmission with floor shifter was available. Later in the year, Dodge released the 180-hp 273-ci V-8 as an option. Darts—GT's and otherwise—were an inexpensive choice of hot rodders trying their hand at the local drag strips.

By the end of 1964, Dodge and Plymouth were firmly rooted in performance. Mopars were becoming performance cars to be reckoned with on the street and the strip. The second half of the sixties would witness the most exciting, powerful and charismatic Dodges and Plymouths ever to cruise the streets and terrorize the drag strips of America.

This 1964 Dodge two-door hardtop is posed in front of the geosphere at the 1964 New York World's Fair. Performance styling was not yet in the Dodge stylists' vocabulary.

CHAPTER THREE

The Barracuda
1964-1969

*T*he Plymouth Barracuda, introduced in May 1964, was an exciting new addition to the Plymouth line. Chrysler designers and engineers employed the "something new, something borrowed" approach. The Barracuda was based on the 106-inch-wheelbase Valiant, sharing all sheetmetal forward of the firewall and below the car's beltline. This hybrid design approach was a good one for the Barracuda—design time and tooling were cut in half and *Road & Track* magazine considered the Valiant to be ". . . one of the best all-around domestic cars . . ."

The Barracuda was a fastback for the masses. Chrysler product planner at the time, Joe Sturm, said, "The Valiant was a fine car for Mr. and Mrs. America, but there was a feeling around the studio that a sportier derivative was needed." The car was not yet targeted for the youth market. Indeed, the brochure for the 1964 Barracuda stated the car was ". . . for people of all ages and interests." Nevertheless, the brochure featured distinctly youthful models.

As conceived, practically all of the fastback was glass, which wrapped down to the fenderline. Planning and sketching at the studio coincided with development of large pieces of automotive glass by Pittsburgh Plate Glass. The result of the collaboration was the largest rear window ever installed on a standard production car up to that time, measuring 14.4 square feet.

The fastback glass design was more than sporty, it was functional. Visibility to the rear was greatly increased—a safety factor. However, the consequent greenhouse effect also raised interior temperatures during sunny days. A carpeted, folding "security panel" separated the interior from the small trunk. By folding the rear seatbacks forward and lowering the security panel, you had an enclosed area seven feet long to carry skis, lumber or other long cargo. A handsome chrome bar prevented cargo from sliding forward into the front passenger seats. These features greatly increased trunk space of the Barracuda.

Before the driver was a rectangular instrument cluster with a matte-silver finish and circular chrome instrument bezels. To the left of the steering column was a speedometer and to the right were the fuel, temperature and ammeter gauges; there was no tachometer. To the left and right of these were the other standard controls. A padded dash was optional, as was a wood-grain steering wheel which, if the brochure was to be believed, gave you the feel of a "racing car."

The interior colors available were gold, red, blue or black. The embossed pleats on the seat cushions were repeated around the door and window controls and armrests. Chromed plastic bands added highlights to the door and quarter panels. Upper door panels were painted metal to match. Just below the vent windows was the Barracuda emblem in chrome script on a field of black. This chrome script was repeated on the front fenders.

The '64 Barracuda came with one of three engines. Standard was a 101-hp 170-ci six-cylinder. The optional engines included a 225-ci six-cylinder with 145 hp and a two-barrel 273-ci V-8 with 180 hp. Optional with these two engines was Chrysler's new four-speed manual transmission with a Hurst linkage. A three-speed manual transmission was standard, as was a 3.23:1 rear axle ratio. Chrysler's new Sure-Grip differential was optional.

The suspension was standard Valiant, with torsion bars up front—a Chrysler tradition—and 2½-inch outboard-mounted asymmetrical leaf springs in the rear. Power brakes were standard, with 9x2½-inch drums up front and 9x2-inch drums in the rear, having a total swept area of 153.5 square inches. The Safety-Rim wheels measured 13x4½ inches mounted with 6.50x13 tires.

The 1964 Barracuda was an excellent example of space utilization. It was available with a 180-hp 273 V-8, four-speed manual transmission and Sure-Grip differential as options.

The '64 Barracuda was available in one of thirteen exterior colors.

Options included the three-speed TorqueFlight automatic transmission, power steering, power brakes, air conditioning, tinted glass (a tinted rear window was standard), a dealer-installed rear window defogger, magnesium-type sport wheel covers with exposed chrome-plated wheel lugs or ribbed wheel covers with simulated knock-off hubs, and numerous other comfort and convenience options.

Base list price with the standard six-cylinder was under $2,500. Despite its mid-year introduction, 25,443 units were sold.

Because new models are typically introduced in the fall, no sooner had the '64 Barracuda been launched when Plymouth issued literature for the 1965 model. There were subtle cosmetic changes reflected in the new brochure, but these were so slight the two brochures were almost identical.

Although heavily based on the Valiant, Plymouth wanted to establish the Barracuda as a distinct model. Consequently, the Valiant chrome script that appeared on the 1964 model's trunk lid was deleted on the 1965 model. For the brochure, this was carefully airbrushed out in all three-quarter-rear views.

For 1965, Barracuda buyers had a choice of two standard engines. The 145-hp six-cylinder or the 180-hp 273 V-8 were now the base engines, and the 273 V-8 was available at no extra cost. Plymouth engineers had been at work pumping up the small-block V-8 engine's output. For '65, you could order the Commando 273 four-barrel V-8 with a respectable 235 hp, as an extra-cost option.

Plymouth had done its homework on the suspension as well. To improve the car's handling, you could order the Rallye Pack suspension, which increased the number of semi-elliptical rear spring leaves and the diameter of the front torsion bars, and included heavy-duty shock absorbers and a 0.82-inch-diameter front stabilizer bar.

To make the buyer's decision of putting together a performance Barracuda a lot easier, Plymouth introduced the Formula S in 1965. This included the Commando 273 V-8 Rallye Pack suspension, wide-rim fourteen-inch wheels mounted with 6.95x14 Goodyear Blue Streak tires, simulated bolt-on wheel covers and a 6000 rpm tachometer. List price for the Formula S was $3,169. A Formula S medallion on the left and right front fenders identified the car. Oddly, the distinctive racing stripe running down the center of the car was optional.

1964 Barracuda.

Road & Track tested the 1965 Barracuda Formula S. With the optional four-speed manual transmission (only $59), the 3,200-pound car accelerated to 60 mph in 8.2 seconds and did the quarter mile in 15.9 seconds at 85 mph. For such a small V-8, this was impressive. In closing, *Road & Track* said, "For those people who enjoy sports car driving but, for reasons of family or business, need four seats and adequate baggage space, the Barracuda would certainly make an excellent compromise." Plymouth had hit the nail squarely on the head!

For 1966, the Barracuda received a facelift and a number of detail changes. Front end sheetmetal and the die-cast metal grille were new, but these made the car look staid compared to the previous model. A stylish new Barracuda medallion depicting the aggressive saltwater fish embellished the grille divider and base of the rear window. Fender-mounted turn signal indicators were new and the taillights were redesigned. A lacquered pinstripe, color coordinated to the interior, ran the length of the car on both sides. Shell-type bucket seats replaced the previous bucket seats. The instrument panel was also new. Interior colors included Citron (gold), tan and white, red, blue and black. There were now seventeen exterior colors. The number of optional racing stripes was upped to six for 1966. New options included a redesigned center console and front disc brakes, but power assist remained optional. The Commando 273 V-8 now came equipped with an unsilenced air cleaner, but performance specifications remained unchanged.

A highly customized and modified 1966 Barracuda played a central role in the 1966 film, *Fireball 500.* The movie starred those darlings of the beach movies, Frankie Avalon, Annette Funicello and Fabian. The car was customized by George Barris of North Hollywood, California. The roof was chopped off, and dual cockpits were formed for just a driver and passenger, with long flared headrests and short, clear plastic windshields. The front and rear ends were extended. The car was powered by a modified 426 Hemi, mated to a four-speed manual transmission. Extra-wide wheels and tires got power to the pavement. Forty coats of hand-rubbed lacquer began with white pearl at the front of the car fading to a gold, then orange, then red and finally burgundy. After the movie was released, the car toured the custom car show circuit and AMT manufactured a model kit of it.

In 1967, Plymouth launched a new ad campaign with the line: "Plymouth is out to win you over," and a red heart with an upturned arrow symbol. To win prospective Barracuda owners over, Plymouth completely redesigned the car and added a hardtop coupe and a convertible. The new Barracuda made a complete break from its Valiant roots and all sheetmetal

With the rear seatback folded forward, carrying capacity was greatly increased in the 1964 Barracuda. Note the superb fit, finish and detailing.

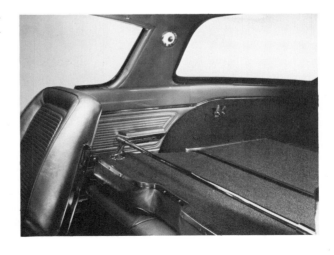

was uniquely its own. Plymouth targeted the second-generation Barracuda directly at the youth market.

In redesigning the fastback Barracuda was longer and wider, but not lower. Wheelbase was extended from 106 inches to 108 inches. Front track increased from 55.9 inches to 57.4 inches, while rear track remained the same at 55.6 inches. Overall length increased from 188.2 inches to 192.8 inches and overall width increased from 70.1 to 71.6 inches. Overall height remained within a fraction of an inch between the first- and second-generation Barracudas, although the new convertible did have a slightly lower roof.

In redesigning the fastback Barracuda, named the Sports Barracuda for 1967, Plymouth aimed for an Italian GT look. The stylists came pretty close. You can see the lines reminiscent of the Maserati Mistral and Ferrari Lusso. The design of the front grille retained the basic identifying features

The Hurst Hemi Under Glass Barracuda pulled some of the most radical wheelstands at drag strips during the early sixties, aided by the rear-mounted engine.

established by earlier Barracuda models. Parking lights, designed in the style of European road lights, were located in the grille. Another European touch was the quick-fill gas cap on the left rear fender, an idea that first appeared on racing cars.

Inside, buyers were greeted to both the new and familiar. A new sports front bench seat with individual backs and a folding center armrest was standard. Newly designed bucket seats were optional. The forward-folding rear seat and security panel conversion feature were retained in the Sports Barracuda. The folding rear seat had a redesigned latch that made it more convenient to lock or release the seat in the up or down position. The catch bar was eliminated for 1967.

Interestingly, in describing the Sports Barracuda, Plymouth made use of the name contraction 'Cuda. This would become a distinct model name later.

This heavily customized 1966 Barracuda appeared in the movie *Fireball 500*. Powered by a modified 426 Hemi, this car was incredibly fast.

The 1966 Barracuda got an exclusive interior not shared with the Valiant. This fish-eye photo shows the optional console with optional TorqueFlight automatic transmission.

The medallion on the front fender identifies this 1966 Barracuda as a Formula S. The 235-hp four-barrel 273 V-8 was the biggest engine offered in the Barracuda that year.

The hardtop offered the more conservative buyer an alternative to the fastback. Its rear window glass had an unusual upward curl along the top that allowed the roof to extend farther back and still provide ample headroom. The hardtop had a conventional trunk. The standard interior appointments were the same as those in the Sports Barracuda. A vinyl roof in a range of colors was optional.

The convertible was welcomed by open-air-driving enthusiasts. The top was power operated and the rear window was glass so the owner wouldn't have to suffer from a clear plastic window aging to a foggy yellow. The convertible's interior was upgraded from that of the fastback and hardtop, having separate bucket seats.

All three Barracuda models had full instrumentation. To the left of the steering column was the 120 mph speedometer. To the right was an

The Barracuda convertible was introduced in 1967. Note the clean lines of the stowed top.

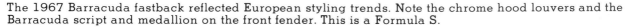

The 1967 Barracuda fastback reflected European styling trends. Note the chrome hood louvers and the Barracuda script and medallion on the front fender. This is a Formula S.

instrument dial the same size as the speedometer, with a gas gauge, temperature gauge, oil pressure gauge and amp gauge. Directly in front of the driver was a smaller-diameter recess that could accept an optional Performance Indicator giving manifold vacuum to let the driver know if he or she was a lead foot (power) or a feather foot (economy). A tachometer could be ordered in place of the Performance Indicator.

Four engines were now offered. The 225-ci six or the two-barrel 273-ci V-8 again offered a choice of standard engines. Optional was the 235-hp four-barrel 273 V-8. The new four-barrel 383 V-8 with 280 hp was optional only in the Formula S Barracuda. For the first time, Plymouth printed actual performance specifications on the back of the 1967 Barracuda brochure. The specifications were so detailed that camshaft duration and lift, valve diameter, tappet clearance and valve spring rates were even listed.

The interior of the 1967 Barracuda showed increased sophistication. The optional four-speed manual transmission and console were installed in this one.

The 1967-69 Barracuda hardtop appealed to the more conservative buyer.

40

You could have your pick of power trains for 1967. While the three-speed manual transmission was standard with most engines, the four-speed manual and TorqueFlight automatic transmissions were of interest to performance enthusiasts. You could dress up the interior with an optional console with the four-speed manual transmission.

The standard rear axle ratio for the hot 273 and 383 V-8's was 3.23:1. Optional Sure-Grip ratios for the 273 V-8 included 3.55:1 and 3.91:1, but the 383 V-8 had no optional ratios, at least from the factory. Higher ratios could be dealer installed. Both performance V-8's came with a beefier 8¾-inch-diameter ring gear regardless of the transmission or standard or optional rear axle ratio, with one exception: The four-barrel 273 V-8 with automatic transmission came standard with a 7¼-inch-diameter ring gear.

The top-of-the-line Formula S package was expanded and improved in a number of ways. The aforementioned 383 V-8 boosted the car's performance considerably. Zero-to-sixty miles per hour was reached in 7.4 seconds and the quarter mile covered in 15.9 seconds. The 383 came with dual exhaust instead of the low-restriction single exhaust used on the four-barrel 273 V-8. Fender plaques announced "383 Four Barrel" to other drivers. Front disc brakes were a mandatory option. The 383 Formula S came with either the four-speed manual or the TorqueFlight automatic transmission and bucket seats with console as part of the package. You could not order air conditioning or power steering with the 383 Formula S due to underhood space limitations.

On the back of the 1967 Barracuda brochure, Plymouth announced the National Barracuda Owner's Club. This was just the tip of the iceberg in Plymouth's (and Dodge's) performance involvement with owners of their cars after the sale.

Plymouth had this to say about its 1968 Barracudas: "Call them unique. They are. The one-of-a-kind sports cars with a zest for the fun life. These are the cars that are coming on strong all over America. The Plymouth win-you-over beat goes on." While the 1968 Barracuda may have defied the traditional definition of a sports car, it definitely met the criteria in performance and handling, with none of the old drawbacks of ". . . rain

The 1967 Barracuda featured a snap-open fuel filler cap.

When the Barracuda was restyled for 1967, the fastback retained the conversion feature of the earlier model.

41

burbling under the windscreen, the heater wheezing at your ankle, and the wind screaming through the leaks in your side-curtains," as one Barracuda ad put it.

For 1968, the Barracuda fastback had a list price of $2,736, the hardtop had a list price of $2,579 and the convertible had a list price of $2,907.

Stylistically, only the front grille and rear taillights were new. There were more substantial changes beneath the skin.

Plymouth expanded the availability of the Formula S package to include the hardtop and convertible. The 273 V-8's were dropped and in their place was a new 230-hp two-barrel 318 V-8 and a 275-hp four-barrel 340 V-8. The high-performance 383 received twenty more horsepower via a new four-barrel intake manifold and cylinder heads so as not to be outdone by the new high-performance 340 V-8. Thus, the Formula S came as either the 340-S or the 383-S. Chrome hood louvers announced the displacement. Handling was improved somewhat with Super Wide Oval Red Streak tires. A wild option on the '68 Barracuda was the red plastic wheelhouse liners. These really stood out on black and dark-blue cars.

Available rear axle ratios were increased. The 340 V-8 came standard with a 3.23:1 ratio. Sure-Grip ratios were available in 3.23:1, 3.55:1 and 3.91:1 with the four-speed manual transmission, and a 3.23:1 or 3.55:1 ratio with the automatic transmission. The 383 V-8 could now have the same Sure-Grip axle and transmission combinations as the new 340.

The suspension was tailored to each specific model. For the standard six-cylinder Barracuda, the front spring rate was eighty-five pounds per inch while the rear springs were 108 pounds per inch. The 318 V-8-equipped Barracuda came with front springs rated at 100 pounds per inch and rear springs rated at 132 pounds per inch. The Formula S 340 came with 103-pounds-per-inch front springs and 132-pounds-per-inch rear springs. The Formula S with the 383 came with 115-pounds-per-inch front springs and 150-pounds-per-inch rear springs. In addition, the Formula S with the 340 had a 0.88-inch-diameter front stabilizer bar which was beefed up to 0.94 inch with the 383. Both Formulas had heavy-duty shock absorbers.

The option list for the '68 Barracuda was a long one. The new Decor Group gave you luxury bucket seats up front and a luxury bench rear seat,

The 1968 Super Stock Hemi Barracudas ran ten-second elapsed times at over 130 mph. These cars were built by Hurst Performance in Michigan and sold through Plymouth dealers for sanctioned drag racing only.

a simulated wood-grain appliqué on door and quarter trim panels, rear armrests with bright bases and ashtrays, carpeted wheel housings in the rear compartment of the fastback and deluxe acceleration, clutch and brake pedals.

You could further dress up the interior with sports-type three-spoke simulated wood-grain steering wheel, sports console, head restraints to match the bucket seats, or a Rallye Cluster Group that included a simulated wood-grain appliqué across the instrument panel, a specially calibrated 150 mph speedometer and a trip odometer.

You had your choice dressing up the outside as well. There were four optional wheelcovers to choose from. Instead of the racing stripes running down the center of the car, now there were Sport Stripes in five colors that ran along the sides. Accent stripes (pinstripes) in five colors followed the upper fenderline.

In 1968, Chrysler contracted with Hurst Performance to build a limited production run of Hemi-powered Dodge Darts and Barracudas, to be sold to drag racers for competition in Super Stock drag racing. It made more sense to have Hurst build these cars than to tie up a Chrysler assembly line. In its small factory in Michigan, Hurst modified the cars to accept the 426 Hemi and added the necessary hardware to withstand the rigors of the quarter-mile strip. The cars were finished in white, to be painted by the buyer as he wished.

One of the most aggressive racers campaigning the 1968 Super Stock Hemi Barracuda was Don Grotheer. That year he was the Super Stock Eliminator runner-up at the NHRA Springnationals. He became the NHRA National Speed and E.T. Record Holder in SS/B and SS/BA classes. That year he joined the Plymouth SuperCar Clinics, speaking around the country on tips for Plymouth performance buffs.

"Look what Plymouth's up to now" was the catch phrase for 1969. The Barracuda received a mild facelift with a new grille. Absent were the chrome hood louvers. The 'Cuda Performance Package was new this year, available on the fastback and hardtop only. Essentially, it was an appearance option with Formula S underpinnings. The package consisted of two hood scoops, two black hood stripes and black lower-body paint treatment all around. You could order a 'Cuda 340 or 'Cuda 383. In either case, it came standard with a four-speed manual transmission with Hurst shifter.

For 1968, the Barracuda interior reached a new level of refinement through the use of handsome vinyl seats and tasteful use of chrome trim.

Besides the graphics package, identification came in the form of 'Cuda 340 or 'Cuda 383 decals behind the front wheelwells.

The Formula S 340 and Formula S 383 were still available on all body styles, identified by a broad racing stripe running the length of the car along the fenderline. This was interrupted just ahead of the doors with either 340 or 383 to announce displacement, a practice that had become *de rigueur* on all performance cars in the late sixties.

There were a number of new appearance options for 1969. Cast aluminum wheels were available on the Barracuda for the first time. Besides the four different color vinyl roofs, there was a new Mod Top—a field of pale flowers that seemed to tie in with the "psychedelia" craze of the late sixties. This garish pattern could also be ordered for the seats and door trim panels. A new leatherlike steering wheel added a European note. You could order your 'Cuda in one of seventeen exterior colors.

Although not mentioned in the 1969 brochure, Plymouth apparently released a 440 'Cuda later in the year. One magazine tested the car. With a curb weight of 3,405 pounds, the 440 'Cuda fastback did 0-60 mph in an astounding 5.6 seconds and the quarter mile in 14.0 seconds.

The list price for the fastback in 1969 was $2,707, the convertible sold for $2,976 and the hardtop went for $2,674.

Don Grotheer had a better year in 1969. He won the Super Stock Eliminator title at the NHRA Winternationals, and was SS/BA class winner as well. At the NHRA Springnationals he was again SS/BA class winner and held the NHRA National E.T. record in that class.

While the Barracuda was approaching its zenith in terms of performance, its body was three years old. It was time for a change—one that Plymouth stylists would handle with supreme ability.

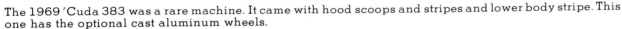

The 1969 'Cuda 383 was a rare machine. It came with hood scoops and stripes and lower body stripe. This one has the optional cast aluminum wheels.

CHAPTER FOUR

The Dodge Dart
1965-1969

*D*uring the last half of the sixties, the Dodge Dart had a distinct performance image advantage over the Plymouth Valiant. When the Plymouth Barracuda was spun off the Valiant, the handsome new fastback stole most of the performance thunder. The Valiant was thus marketed as an economical compact, even though the V-8's and the four-speed manual transmission were available. The Dodge Dart, on the other hand, had no such derivative model, and Dodge could concentrate solely on the Dart GT and other Dart performance models to build its compact performance image.

The 1965 Dodge Dart GT had begun to capture the attention of performance enthusiasts. Dart sheetmetal was unchanged from 1964, but the hood, front grille, rear end and taillights were new.

Identifying a 1965 Dart GT was difficult because it was low-key. In 1964, the small letters GT appeared on the hood, on the sides of the convertible and the rear roof pillars of the hardtop, as well as on the insides of the doors. There were no such exterior markings on the 1965 Dart GT. Instead, there were three bogus vents on the rocker panels, just behind the front wheelwells.

Identification could be helped by ordering an optional racing stripe running from the front of the hood to the rear, on the driver's side.

Inside, the driver was greeted by premium-line bucket seats, with a pleated and diamond accent design with chrome trim. The entire interior was vinyl with full carpeting.

The three-speed manual column shift was standard. Gone was the optional push-button automatic transmission. Dart GT buyers who selected an automatic transmission in 1965 received a floor-mounted selector lever that came with its own short console. The optional manual four-speed transmission came with a decorative, die-cast floor plate.

The 1965 Dart GT still came standard with the 170-ci slant six. The optional 225-ci six helped matters a bit. Those in a hurry ignored the sixes and checked the 273-ci V-8. For 1965, the 273 received a dramatic increase in power, pumping out 235 hp.

One test of the Dart GT hardtop with the 235-hp V-8 produced a 0-60 mph time of 9.3 seconds with a quarter-mile time of 16.4 seconds.

Not all of Dodge's drag racing efforts centered on the mid-size cars. The Dart benefited as well. For 1965, Dodge arranged with a company called Fibercraft to produce complete fiberglass body panels for the Dart.

Replacing the steel body with the fiberglass body eliminated nearly 400 pounds from the car—a real plus for drag racers.

The Dart was significantly restyled for 1966. Front end sheetmetal was all new. Rear end sheetmetal remained the same, but detailing of the taillights and trim panel in between was new. The rear bumper was larger.

The GT's identification was altered for 1966. The bogus vents of 1965 were gone. The entire length of the rocker panels on the 1966 Dart GT received chrome trim, and there was more chrome trim atop the fenders. A wildly symbolic GT medallion on the rear fenders just before the word Dart distinguished the car from other Darts.

Inside, the facings of the front bucket and rear bench seats were new. There was also a new optional center console used with the automatic and four-speed manual transmissions.

The 1965 Dart GT could be identified by the three bogus vents on the rocker panels. The chrome mag wheels on this convertible were installed by the owner.

Four-speed manual-transmission-equipped Dart GT's came with a die-cast floor plate. Automatic transmissions came with a short console and selector lever.

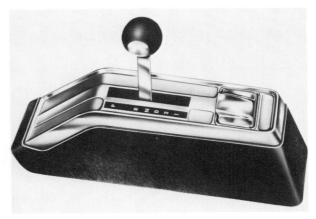

All standard and optional engines and drivetrain components continued unchanged for 1966.

Despite the Dart's restyling over the previous few years, the car was beginning to show its age. In 1967, Dodge corrected that.

Dart buyers in 1967 were introduced to a crisp, contemporary new car inside and out. Wheelbase remained at 111 inches. This was a selling

The 1966 Dart GT interior had show-car-like styling which helped to make the Dart one of the most popular compacts on the market.

The 1966 Dart GT could be identified by the stylish medallion on the rear fenders. The wheel covers were unique to the Dart GT.

point in the Dart: "Looking for an Escape from Cramped Compacts? Lots of people are. That's why Dart—the Dodge-sized compact—gives you instant relief from compacts that are too small."

As for the Dart GT, no longer did it try to hide its light under a basket. A rectangular medallion on the front fenders read Dart GT. A same-size medallion with just GT was mounted in the center of the grille.

Inside, the biggest change was to the dash. It was redesigned and bore a resemblance to the Dart's bigger brother, the Charger. The bucket seats were standard in the GT hardtop. The GT convertible came standard with a front bench seat; bucket seats were optional. The center console was optional on both GT hardtop and convertible.

The Dart GT was available in eighteen standard acrylic enamel colors. A special, buffed silver-metallic paint was offered as an option. An optional black or white Levant-grain vinyl roof handsomely set off the paint color.

There were four engines available in the Dart GT for 1967. The standard 170-ci one-barrel six received a boost in power, to 115 hp. The optional one-barrel 225-ci six was still rated at 145 hp. The two V-8's were the 180-hp two-barrel 273 and the 235-hp four-barrel 273. Announcing engine displacement somewhere on the front fenders or hood was becoming the norm among performance cars. With the four-barrel 273, the Dart GT received a medallion on the front fenders stating just that.

All the transmission offerings remained the same, but the sixes equipped with automatic transmissions had a new "partial kickdown" (second-gear) feature for improved acceleration for passing.

Besides the V-8 engines, there were other performance-related options for the 1967 Dart GT's. These included a console-mounted ta-

In 1967 the Dart received a handsome new body. These GT models had the 273-ci four-barrel.

chometer on V-8-powered GT's only, heavy-duty shock absorbers, a faster 16:1 manual steering ratio, front disc brakes, D70x14-inch Red Streak nylon cord tires and wide-rim (5.5J) wheels.

To improve the Dart's handling and braking in one package, Dodge offered the Dart Rallye option. This included front disc brakes, heavy-duty rear springs, heavy-duty torsion bars, antisway bar, D70x14-inch Red Streak tires and wide-rim wheels.

A less comprehensive handling option was the Rallye Suspension Package. This included heavy-duty torsion bars, heavy-duty ball joints, heavy-duty rear springs and antisway bar.

The 1968 Dart GTS was a new model. A 300-hp 383 V-8 was the biggest optional engine, available only in the GTS.

One of the optional wheel covers on the 1968 Dart was this simulated magnesium design. The simulated wood sports steering wheel with padded hub was a popular option on the 1968 Dart.

With so much performance hardware to back it up, the Dart became a prime mover in the Sports Car Club of America's (SCCA) new Sedan Class racing series. For racing in this series, the compact cars, which also included Ford Falcons and Plymouth Barracudas as well as foreign makes, were prepared like stock cars on the NASCAR Grand National circuit. "Baby Grands" was the nickname coined for these cars. Darts were powered by the four-barrel 273 V-8 and were equipped with full roll cages and fifteen-inch wheels with fat tires. Bob Tullius, long famous for his Quaker State Motor Oil Group 44-marked cars, was one of the first to drive the Dodge Dart in the Sedan Class, and with notable success.

Dodge announced the Scat Pack for 1968, and the Dart benefited by being a member of the family. While there were minor cosmetic changes, the biggest news was in performance.

The 1968 Dart had a new optional V-8: the 230-hp two-barrel 318-ci V-8.

The 1968 Dart GT hardtop had a list price of $2,611, and the GT convertible sold for $2,831.

A new higher-performance model—the GTS—was added to the Dart line. The GTS was available as a hardtop for $3,163 and as a convertible for $3,383. In print, Dodge called it the GTSport.

The GTS was distinguished by vented hood power bulges. Also setting off the GTS were body side racing stripes. At no extra cost, you could choose instead bumblebee stripes that wrapped around the rear end of the car. The bumblebee stripes were available in red, black or white. You could also choose to have no stripes at all. GTS identification appeared on the hood, sides of the front fenders and the trunk lid.

The interior appointments and colors of the GTS were essentially the same as the GT, as were the exterior colors. Vinyl-covered bucket seats were standard on the Dart GT and GTS hardtops. The GT and GTS convertibles featured vinyl-covered bench seats as standard, but vinyl-covered bucket seats were available as an option.

The GTS was at the top of the Dart line. It was offered with two V-8's that were available on the GTS and no other Dodge model. A 275-hp four-barrel 340-ci V-8 was standard. Incredibly, a 300-hp 383 V-8 was optional.

Dodge did a super job on the GTS exhaust system. The 340 GTS and the 383 GTS came with 2¼-inch-diameter exhaust pipes and tail pipes for a low-restriction system. Both dual exhaust systems used tuned mufflers and chrome exhaust tips as a finishing touch.

Vinyl bucket seats were standard in the GT and GTS hardtops and optional in the GT and GTS convertibles for 1968.

The three-speed manual column shift was standard on all Dart models. It was out of keeping on the GTS, and most of those buyers ordered the high-upshift, competition-type TorqueFlight automatic transmission or the four-speed manual transmission with Hurst Competition-Plus floor shift with simulated wood-grain knob and reverse-engagement warning light.

With the 275-hp 340 V-8 the GTS could reach 60 mph in six seconds and cover the quarter mile in just over fifteen seconds. The optional 300-hp 383 transformed the GTS into a land rocket, but it did not handle quite as well as the 340-V-8-equipped GTS because of the greater weight on the front wheels. The 383 GTS was really a straight-line machine.

Speaking of handling, the GTS came standard with the Rallye Suspension. This included heavy-duty torsion bars (0.88-inch diameter for the 340 GTS, 0.94-inch diameter for the 383 GTS), heavy-duty ball joints, heavy-duty rear springs with six leaves each, heavy-duty shock absorbers and antisway bar. Also standard on the GTS were E70x14 Red Streak tires mounted on 14x5.5J wide-rim wheels. With these wheels and tires, the GTS had a slightly wider track than that of the other Dart models. The deep-dish simulated "mag" wheelcovers were standard on the GTS and optional on other Dart models if ordered with the 5.5J wide-rim wheels.

The 1968 Darts had an extensive list of options, most carried over from 1967. Among the worthwhile choices were the wood-grain steering wheel with padded hub, tachometer on V-8-equipped models with center console, power steering and brakes, faster 16:1 manual steering, color-keyed head restraints for the front seats and vinyl roofs in three colors.

Although big-name drag racers like Dick Landy and Don Garlits had modified Darts in the mid-sixties to run in the NHRA Funny Car class using 426 Hemi power, Super Stock class racing of the Dart was almost non-existent due to the small V-8's available. To solve this, Dodge contracted

The hood bulges on the 1969 Dart Swinger 340 and GTS announced what was under the hood.

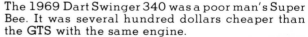

The 1969 Dart Swinger 340 was a poor man's Super Bee. It was several hundred dollars cheaper than the GTS with the same engine.

with Hurst Performance of Michigan in 1968 to build a limited number of 440 wedge- and 426 Hemi-powered Darts to compete in SS/B. These cars would successfully cover the quarter mile with elapsed times in the ten-second range. According to Chrysler staff engineer Larry Shepard, the majority of these Darts were Hemi-powered, although a small pilot run of fifty 440-powered Darts was also built in 1968. "In 1969," said Shepard, "we built over 600 440-powered Darts—basically the same as the 383 GTS, except for the engine."

There were nine Dart models to choose from in 1969. The Dart GT and GTSport were joined by a new member of the Dodge Scat Pack—the Dart Swinger 340.

This new car was designed to offer you the most for your performance compact dollar. It had less luxury than the GTS but just as much scat. It came standard with the 340-ci four-barrel V-8, four-speed manual transmission with Hurst shifter, three-spoke steering wheel with padded hub, Rallye suspension, bumblebee stripes with the word Swinger, performance hood and D70x14 wide tread tires on 5.5J wheels. List price for the Swinger 340 hardtop was less than $2,900. By comparison, the GTS hardtop cost $3,226 with the same standard engine. The GTS convertible cost $3,419.

The Dart Swinger, including the Swinger 340, was available in seventeen exterior colors. Optional vinyl roofs were black, white, green antique or tan. A pleated, all-vinyl interior was optional, if you found the standard all-vinyl interior too plain. Full carpeting was standard in the Swinger 340 with the standard four-speed manual transmission, but optional when the TorqueFlight automatic transmission was ordered.

Without question, the sleeper of the 1969 Dodge Scat Pack was the Dart GTS equipped with the optional 383 four-barrel V-8. This engine had received a boost in performance and was now rated at 330 hp, just five fewer horsepower than the 383 V-8 used in the heavier Coronet Super Bee.

Straight-line performance of the Dart GT, Swinger 340 and the GTS could be improved by replacing the standard 3.23:1 rear axle with a 3.55:1

The standard vinyl interior of the 1969 Dart GT and GTS hardtop was more exciting than the year before. The optional TorqueFlight automatic transmission and console are installed in this one.

The bumblebee stripe on the 1969 Dart GTSport (shown) and Swinger 340 looked like this.

or 3.91:1 optional ratio. These higher numerical axle ratios were available at no extra cost if you also ordered the Sure-Grip differential.

By the end of the sixties, the Dart was a full-blown performance car in its own right. It was poised at the threshold of the seventies ready to take on all compact rivals. Interestingly, it was about to get some competition from Plymouth's Rapid Transit System in the form of the Duster.

The 1969 GTS was distinguished by a new grille and taillight panel. A 330-hp 383 was optional for the first time.

CHAPTER FIVE

The Charger 1966-1970

*"T*he Dodge Rebellion wants you!" These were the words of beautiful blonde Pam Austin, heard in millions of living rooms across America during 1966 in one of Dodge's most successful TV campaigns. Miss Austin was the first in a series of eye-catching representatives for Dodge cars into the early seventies. Dodge indeed was rebelling from its market perception of offering powerful cars with rather staid styling.

The Dodge Charger of 1966 was tangible evidence of this new thinking. Its styling was the embodiment of that exciting new image. Dodge christened the Charger "The Leader of the Dodge Rebellion"—its performance flagship.

The Charger and Coronet shared the same platform and, hence, dimensions. Wheelbase was 117 inches, width was 75.3 inches, and front and rear treads were 59.5 and 58.5 inches, respectively. The Charger was a fraction of an inch longer at 203.6 inches. As a whole, the Charger's styling (and that of the Coronet) for 1966 represented a quantum leap over that of the 1965 models. The styling of both cars was much crisper than the rather conservative, ambiguous designs of the previous year. The Charger and Coronet shared front end and side sheetmetal, but the addition of the fastback totally altered the Charger's overall look and character. Dodge was aiming the Charger at a younger and more aggressive buyer than that of the Coronet.

Detail differences included larger rear wheel openings on the Charger compared to the Coronet's fender-skirted look. An uncluttered grille running the full width of the car was achieved using retractable headlights and concealed turn signals. The theme was repeated at the rear with a full-width taillight. Charger was spelled out across the one-piece taillight bezel.

The edges of the fastback roofline were raised slightly, and the left and right edges of the rear window were curled up accordingly. Charger was again spelled out in chrome script on the sides of the fastback.

The interior was one of the most exciting and well-thought-out designs of the sixties. There were four padded, stitched vinyl bucket seats. The front and rear seats were separated by a full-length console. Courtesy lights were positioned on the console forward of the front seats. A padded armrest was mounted to the console for the driver and passenger. The rear seating borrowed a concept from the 1964 Barracuda. The rear seatbacks and the armrest separating them could be folded forward; dropping the hinged trunk panel separating the trunk from the interior, and opening the trunk lid, you then had an area four-by-seven-and-a-half feet long. With the 1966 Charger, you didn't need roof racks to carry long items such as skis or lumber. It's one of the best examples of space utilization to come out of Detroit. Complementing the interior appointments was a tasteful blend of brushed aluminum and chrome trim on the console, doors and rear quarter panels.

The dash, by comparison, was almost too busy, resembling a Buck Rogers instrument panel of brushed chrome dials, knobs and switches. There were four main circular instruments before the driver. The first on the left gave alternator and gas readings. A 150 mph speedometer was next. A 6000 rpm tachometer was next to the speedometer. And the fourth instrument gave water temperature and oil pressure. No idiot lights here! For those who always forgot to put on their watch, there was an optional console-located electric clock. A thoughtful touch: The hood release was now mounted on the dash, along with the other routine controls.

There were four engines to choose from. Standard was the venerable 318-ci two-barrel V-8 having 230 hp. The optional engines included a 361-ci two-barrel V-8 with 265 hp, a 383-ci four-barrel V-8 with dual exhaust and 325 hp and, finally, Chrysler's new 426-ci street Hemi V-8 with dual four-barrel carburetors, sewer-sized dual exhaust, with 425 hp.

Transmissions were matched to their powerplants and intended use. The 318 got a three-on-the-tree manual transmission. Choosing the 361, 383 or 426 Hemi necessitated the three-speed TorqueFlight automatic or four-on-the-floor manual transmission, both at extra cost—hence the term "mandatory option." The 318 could be ordered with the optional TorqueFlight, but not the four-speed. The warranty for the 318, 361 and 383 V-8's and their transmissions was for five years or 50,000 miles. The 426 Hemi had a reduced warranty of twelve months or 12,000 miles. Although one of its strongest engines, Chrysler knew Hemi owners would more than likely thrash their cars unmercifully. Thus, the Hemi warranty was only valid, as stated on the Charger brochure, ". . . provided the car is not subjected to any extreme operation [i.e., drag racing] or the engine or driveline modified in any manner." In other words, if you took it to the strip within the first year of ownership, the warranty was invalidated.

The 1966-67 Charger was an excellent blend of performance and practicality. With its large cargo area, it was almost a fastback station wagon. The 426 Hemi was the top engine offered.

Because of its size and weight, the 1966 Charger wasn't the best handler, but then, Detroit's suspension tuning was in its infancy compared to today. Bias-belted tires were the norm in the sixties, and these were the biggest limiting factor in a car's handling. The Charger did come with a front antisway bar. Handling could be improved, at the expense of ride, by ordering the optional heavy-duty suspension package with higher-rate springs and shocks front and rear. The Charger rode on 7.75x14 blackwall tires. Hemi-equipped cars were shod with 7.75x14 Blue Streak tires, and came with larger brakes and the heavy-duty suspension as part of the Hemi option.

Many of the 1966 Charger's standard items have already been listed that made up the car's base list price of just over $3,000. There were sixteen exterior colors to choose from. Interior colors included blue, saddle tan, red, white, citron gold and black.

Among the options were power steering, power brakes, Sure-Grip differential, air conditioning (which was not available with the 361 V-8 with four-speed manual transmission or the 426 Hemi), electric windows, tinted glass, mag-type wheelcovers, trailer-towing package, white sidewall tires and front and rear bumper guards.

NASCAR drivers have always been the first to jump on a new car design if it shows promise. The fastback Charger did indeed look promising for the 1966 Grand National stock car season. The Charger proved to be a bit tricky on the high-banked ovals at full speed, but the addition of a small rear spoiler corrected the handling problems. Dodge won only two Grand National races in 1965, but by the end of the 1966 NASCAR season, Dodge had won eighteen races, taking the Manufacturers Championship. Plymouth was a close second with sixteen wins. Ford was a distant third with ten wins.

On the USAC circuit, Norm Nelson was so successful racing his Plymouth that he won eighteen races and the title. Dodge won only eight; it is difficult to determine if these wins were all by Chargers or were shared with Coronets.

The Charger was somewhat of an unknown quantity on the NHRA and AHRA (American Hot Rod Association) rosters for 1966. Besides, aero-

The 1967 Charger had a shortened optional center console with a fixed center cushion. A fold-down center armrest for the front seat was also optional, permitting three to sit up front.

dynamics were less of an issue in drag racing, where horsepower has always ruled. In fact, Dodge's most visible proponent, Dick Landy, shunned the Charger in favor of the Coronet in 1966 and 1967.

For 1967, Dodge didn't try to top itself, it merely made a good thing better. Stylistically, the Charger was unaltered, but there were two important interior changes. The center console was now optional. Also, instead of running between both front and rear seats, the console was shortened —stopping just behind the front seats. This made it easier for rear passengers to choose which door to exit at curbside. If you didn't want the front console, you could order a fixed center cushion with fold-down armrest between the front seats, permitting three to sit up front when needed.

The other big piece of news was the availability of the 375-hp 440-ci four-barrel Magnum V-8. Charger buyers could now get near-Hemi-like performance at a substantial saving on purchase price and insurance premiums, with the added bonus of Chrysler's five-year, 50,000-mile warranty. Enthusiast magazines tested both 440 V-8 and 426 Hemi Chargers. The 440 Charger did 0-60 mph in 8.0 seconds and the quarter mile in 15.5 seconds—rather slow times due to poor driving. The 426 Hemi Charger did 0-60 mph in 6.4 seconds and the quarter mile in 14.2 seconds.

The 440 Magnum wasn't the only news from the engine compartment for 1967. The 318 V-8 was now sixty pounds lighter thanks to new, lightweight casting techniques as well as a redesigned, lightweight cylinder head that featured wedge combustion chambers like those used in the 440 Magnum. Horsepower remained unchanged, however.

The number of standard exterior colors was increased to eighteen, as well as an optional buffed silver-metallic. Body paint stripe in blue, white, black or red was also standard. Interior colors were now blue, red, copper, black, white/black or gold/black. Vinyl roof covering was a new option, and could be ordered in black or white.

The second-generation Dodge Charger, built between 1968 and 1970, was the finest realization of performance styling in the Charger's history.

Richard Petty was a major force during the NASCAR season of 1967, and for that reason Plymouth was the winning make in Grand National stock car racing that year. Dodge won only five races. (This would change drastically with the introduction of the slippery 1968 Charger.) The 1967 Charger got more publicity on the USAC circuit, thanks to Don White, who won nine races and the title in his Charger.

The 1966-67 Charger marked Dodge's first concerted effort to build up styling and interior appointments as key elements of the car's performance image. Brute horsepower alone was no longer relied upon to entice performance-minded buyers. Dodge did not rest on its laurels, and set out to make the 1968 Charger an even more desirable car.

Bill Brownlie was chief of design of the Dodge studio at the time of the second-generation Charger's gestation. Brownlie had this to say about the car: "I wanted to launch into something much more sporty and extremely aerodynamic in image and function than the 1967 model . . . something extremely masculine that looked like it had just come off the track at Daytona." Due to its tremendous success in NASCAR racing, Chrysler had the desire to design and market a full-size, four-passenger two-door coupe that visually embodied this racing success.

Brownlie put the styling studio to a contest, using one-eighth-scale models to visualize the concept. He had one major stipulation: "I wanted the car to look like the cab sitting on top of the lower body shell, a cockpit-type appearance in conjunction with a tapering down in front, the swelling of the sheetmetal over the front wheels, the pinching of the waist, and the rapid swelling over the rear wheels, both in plan view and side view." Although Dodge had no full-size wind tunnel, aerodynamic engineers on

The 1968 Charger remains a splendid performance styling statement—one of the best-looking muscle cars of the sixties.

the staff made necessary recommendations to the styling team. The final design chosen by Brownlie and Charles Mitchell, who was in charge of pulling the Charger program together, was done by Richard Sias.

The body itself was a direct interpretation of the stated design stipulation. The bulges at the front and rear wheels gave physical meaning to the words muscle car, which originally referred only to a car's horsepower. The most notable things about the body were the sharp edges and the subtle transition of these bulges that made it look as if it were machined out of one block of steel.

The cab that Brownlie spoke of was instrumental in the achievement of an aerodynamic look. As with the body, the roof of a car in the design development stage can consist of infinitely variable compound curves. This was critical with the Charger because of its inherent design concept. In the end, a designer has to choose which combination of curves will be used. Often it is strictly intuitive—what he personally feels is visually correct. On the 1968 Charger, the rear roof pillars swept back in a flying buttress configuration with a sharp trailing edge that beautifully set off the flat recessed rear window. The line interface between the windows and the roof broke slightly at the vertical door line before running down to the body.

This Charger was one of the few designs where a vinyl roof enhanced the appearance. It was most dramatic when a black vinyl roof was ordered with brilliant red or yellow paint. A white vinyl roof contrasted best with dark body colors.

Certain details contributed to the 1968 Charger's racetrack appearance. The concealed headlights were carried over from the previous model, and the entire grille was blacked out; this resembled the taped-over headlights of stock cars. Another racer-bred detail was the quick-fill gas cap on the driver's side. It was originally conceived for both sides, using a saddle-type gas tank to facilitate fillup regardless of which side of the pump the driver pulled up on. Unfortunately, it was scrapped due to cost cutting. The large hood scallops—reminiscent of those used on the Chevrolet Corvette a few years before—had optional turn indicators. This scallop detail was repeated on the doors.

Standard equipment in the 1968 Charger included a fully padded armrest and a European sports-car-type map pocket. A left, outside mirror remote-control was optional.

The instrument panel in the 1968 Charger was designed to look like an aircraft cockpit. The combination clock/tachometer was optional.

The result of this unbridled enthusiasm and attention to detail was and still is an aesthetic triumph. It was successful because the original design platform was adhered to. There were no abrupt changes in the sheet-metal. The design was literally smooth and consistent from nose to tail.

Car and Driver had this to say about the '68 Charger: ". . . the new Charger is beautiful. It looks like a real racer, it's all guts and purpose, and —unlike the Mako Shark-inspired '68 Corvette, it's completely fresh and unexpected." Bill Brownlie was right on the money.

Dodge had a new phrase for this excitement: Dodge Fever! "Down the road slips a new low shape, and you can feel the Fever setting in. The more you look, the harder you fall. For Charger. Every man's dream. Wearing the shape of tomorrow and a price tag that means you can have it today. Watch it, you're getting Dodge Fever . . . and there's only one cure. Charger." [1968 Dodge Charger brochure] Enthusiasts will recall the white-mini-skirted, vivacious brunette in the Dodge Fever ads. Her name was Joan Parker.

By comparison, the interior of the '68 Charger was more subdued than earlier models. The front and rear seats were flat, almost plain, with only a "split hide" detail on the seat faces. Dodge erroneously called them bucket seats, but there was no lumbar support to speak of to hold you during handling maneuvers. The doors featured map pockets for various odds and ends. The new padded dash was a vast improvement with an efficient, no-nonsense appearance, like that of an aircraft cockpit. The instrument panel was matte-black with six instruments tastefully trimmed with chrome: clock, speedometer, fuel, temperature, oil pressure and alternator. A clock/tachometer was optional. The rest of the controls were handsome chrome rocker or thumbwheel switches. The slide controls for the optional air conditioning were integrated with the heater controls to the right of the steering column underneath the instrument panel. A new speed control located on the end of the turn signal lever was optional.

With its exciting new shape and all the standard features buyers had come to expect in a Charger, you got a lot of car for the base list price of $3,014 with standard six-cylinder engine. But few could stop there. Invariably, prospective buyers really caught Dodge Fever and heavily optioned their Chargers.

The gas cap and raised rear lip on the 1968 Charger were race-car-inspired.

The heaviest option you could order was the Charger R/T. Included in the $3,480 R/T package was the 375-hp 440 Magnum V-8, TorqueFlight automatic transmission, heavy-duty manually adjusted brakes, F70x14 Goodyear Red Streak tires, R/T handling package with larger-diameter front torsion bars, extra-heavy-duty rear springs (with an extra half-leaf in the right rear to control torque steer), heavy-duty shocks and the standard front antisway bar. Bumblebee stripes in black or white encircled the rear end; these stripes could be deleted if you wished. R/T medallions were mounted in the grille and rear taillight recess. The four-speed manual transmission was, of course, optional. The Hemi was available only on the Charger R/T, not on the plain Charger.

The '68 Charger R/T was a stunning performer. With a power-to-weight ratio of 10.1 pounds per horsepower, it did 0-60 mph in 6.5 seconds and the quarter mile in the low-fourteen-second range.

If you didn't want so much power under your right foot, you could order the Charger with the 290-hp two-barrel 383 or the newly improved 330-hp four-barrel 383. Chrysler engineers had redesigned the cylinder heads and intake manifold with ten percent larger intakes, unsilenced dual-snorkel air cleaner and low-restriction dual exhaust. This produced 425 pounds-feet of torque at a useful 3200 rpm. It was an excellent powerplant.

The '68 Charger had show to match its go. Striking color combinations could be had with the sixteen standard exterior colors (silver metallic was optional) and optional black, antique white or antique green vinyl roof. Two optional wheelcovers were available as well as the ever-handsome deep-dish, chromed mag-type road wheels. You could better listen to your favorite sounds on the new AM radio/8-track stereo player with three instrument-panel-mounted speakers for "orchestra shell" fidelity.

The story of the '68 Charger on the NASCAR racetracks was both good and bad. The good news was the new Charger was indeed faster than the previous model, hitting 184 mph on the Daytona track. The bad news came from Ford and Mercury. The fastback Ford Torino and Mercury Cyclone were five miles per hour faster than the Charger due to the carburetor restrictors on the Hemi. Dodge won only five of the forty-nine Grant National races during 1968, while Ford captured the checkered flag in twenty races. There were only two ways to make the Charger go faster: come up with a completely new race engine—a prohibitive venture that would have cost millions of dollars—or improve the car's aerodynamics even more.

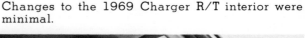
Changes to the 1969 Charger R/T interior were minimal.

Wind tunnel testing of the Charger in one-eighth scale showed excessive turbulence, and thus drag, in the tunnel backlight, and the recessed front grille trapped air getting around the front end. By flushing up the grille and rear window, the turbulence was eliminated. Chargers with these modifications went five miles per hour faster on Chrysler's Chelsea, Michigan, test track. This was a dramatic improvement, achieved without major bodywork alterations.

To qualify as a production car under NASCAR rules, 500 Chargers with these modifications had to be built and sold to the public. Because of the limited number of cars to be built, Dodge felt it would be impractical to tie up its production line to hand-modify each car. Instead, it contracted Creative Industries in Detroit to do the work. The grille from the '68 Coronet fit perfectly in the Charger grille cavity, and was mounted flush. The rear window was moved up to match the angle of the trailing edge of the rear roof pillars, and a fiberglass plug fit below and blended in. To accomplish this, the trunk lid had to be shortened, hinges relocated and a new interior rear shelf fabricated. Identification was provided by a broad racing stripe wrapped around the rear end of the car, with 500 on the sides. The 426 Hemi was the standard and only engine. You could choose between a Torque-Flight or four-speed manual transmission. The suspension was the same as on the other Hemi Chargers. Because the project was begun late in 1968, the Charger 500 was sold as a 1969 model, and competition versions raced that year.

Because of its unique character, Dodge had this to say about the Charger 500 in a 1969 brochure: "... the Charger 500 is offered specifically

The rare 1969 Charger 500 had a flush grille and backlight to improve aerodynamics for racing. The 426 Hemi was the only engine offered in the Charger 500.

for the high-performance race track. It is available only to qualified performance participants and is being built to special order on a limited production basis." With this teaser, coupled with the car's rarity (knowing you would have the only one in your county), enthusiasts poured into dealerships in droves—which, of course, was exactly what Dodge wanted.

Popular Hot Rodding tested both an automatic and manual transmission Charger 500 in 1969, with 3.23:1 rear cogs. The automatic-transmission-equipped car did the quarter mile in 14.01 seconds at 100 mph. The four-speed-equipped car did much better: The quarter-mile elapsed time was 13.60 seconds at 107.44 mph—using street tires! Not bad for a car that weighed over 4,100 pounds.

If your dealer had sold his allotment of Charger 500's, the mass-produced Chargers were plentiful. The '69 model received some cosmetic work. Car spotters could distinguish a '69 from a '68 by the new louvered grille divider. The four round taillights were superseded by two rectangular

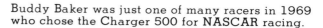

Buddy Baker was just one of many racers in 1969 who chose the Charger 500 for NASCAR racing.

Changes to the 1969 Charger included a new grille divider, taillights and side-marker lights. On R/T's, the bumblebee stripe was now one band instead of two.

recessed bezels. The side-marker lights were also new. Inside, the Charger got new bucket seats.

There were new options, too. The Dodge Custom-Comfort seat could manually adjust to more than 100 seating positions. There was a new fifteen-inch cast aluminum road wheel also.

A new model was added to the Charger lineup in 1969: Charger SE (for Special Edition). This included genuine leather seat facing on the front bucket seats, simulated wood-grain steering wheel, deep-dish wheel-covers, hood-mounted turn signal indicators, simulated wood-grain-finish instrument panel trim and an extensive Light Group. The SE package could also be ordered on the Charger R/T.

Sales for the Charger R/T totaled 20,057 units, up from 17,582 units in 1968.

No sooner had Dodge hit the NASCAR circuit with the Charger 500 than Ford got to work to make its cars more aerodynamic also. Within months, Ford and its Mercury division announced the Torino Talladega and Mercury Cyclone Spoiler in answer to the Charger 500; Dodge lost its speed advantage. Dodge engineers had to go back to the drawing boards and wind tunnels to make the Charger 500 go still faster.

Because of the aerodynamic advantage of the Ford cars, Richard Petty deserted Plymouth and raced a Torino. For that reason, Ford won twenty-six of the fifty-four Grand National races in 1969, while Plymouth won only two. Dodge, however, did quite well with its Charger 500's and won twenty-two Grand National races that year. Still, Chrysler was determined to win the Grand National title with its Charger, and went back into the wind tunnel.

Months of design and testing resulted in probably the most visually striking car ever to come out of Detroit. An eighteen-inch fiberglass bullet

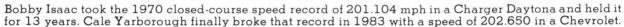

Bobby Isaac took the 1970 closed-course speed record of 201.104 mph in a Charger Daytona and held it for 13 years. Cale Yarborough finally broke that record in 1983 with a speed of 202.650 in a Chevrolet.

nose, reverse-facing scoops on the top of the front fenders (for tire clearance due to the lowered front end) and, for down force, a fully aerodynamic rear spoiler mounted two feet above the rear deck all served to set this car apart from anything else on the street.

The test car, or "mule," with these modifications exceeded 200 mph on Chrysler's Chelsea, Michigan, Proving Grounds. Dodge had itself a winner. Again, 500 street versions had to be built to qualify it as a production car; Creative Industries was again tapped to build them. The car was named after the premier NASCAR track where it would debut: Daytona. Production Charger R/T's were trucked to Creative Industries for conversion, at the rate of seven per day. Production began in early June 1969. The first Daytona was shipped to a Kingston, Ontario, Canada, dealer on June 27, 1969. The 500th Daytona was shipped to Lafayette Dodge in Lafayette, Indiana, on September 8, 1969. There may have been one or two other Daytonas built.

The Daytona was an unmatched success on the NASCAR tracks. It was the fastest stock car in the world. Bobby Isaac established the then world closed-course speed record of 201.104 mph. Daytonas swept their namesake track race winning first, second, third and fourth places. Bobby Isaac was the fastest and most successful driver in his K&K Insurance-sponsored Daytona, and he won the Grand National Championship. Then Isaac took the car to the Bonneville Salt Flats and set four unlimited world records.

The production Charger Daytona was built in the summer of 1969; there was no 1970 model. Bobby Isaac is behind the wheel of the prototype Daytona at Chrysler's Chelsea, Michigan, Proving Grounds. Note his adjustable wing.

Riding on the tide of its racing success, Dodge introduced the regular production 1970 Charger with only minor changes. Most notable was the front chrome loop bumper, which gave the Charger a more formal look. Dodge succeeded in lowering the base price for the Charger to $3,001 by substituting a bench seat for the bucket seats (now optional), eliminating the door pockets, using simpler window moldings and making the electric clock optional.

Dodge offered a 500 model in 1970, but it did not have the flush back-light or grille, and the Hemi was not standard. The Charger 500 was powered that year by the standard 318 V-8 and included bucket seats, electric clock, wheel-lip moldings, and 500 medallions in the front grille and rear taillight recess. It essentially had the features of the basic Charger of 1969. Its list price was $3,139.

The top-of-the-line Charger was, again, the R/T with a list price of $3,711. Specifications remained the same, but there was a new engine available: the 390-hp 440 Six-Pack. There were appearance changes to the Charger R/T in 1970. A flat, reverse-facing scoop with an R/T medallion covered the scallops on the doors. Your R/T stood out by having a choice of either bumblebee stripe or longitudinal tape stripe that followed the body contours and around the reverse scoop on the doors.

Inside, the Charger 500 and R/T had new seats that could truly be called buckets. These seats were available in all-vinyl in blue, green, tan, charcoal black, burnt orange, and white and black. The same bucket seats were also available in cloth-and-vinyl, but only in charcoal black. The bucket seats could be ordered with an optional center cushion with fold-down armrest or a center console. The SE package was carried over for 1970. The radical four-speed shift lever was replaced with a new pistol-grip shifter. A new option on the Charger was the electrically operated steel sun roof; you had to order a vinyl roof to go with it.

The 1970 Charger shared some exterior colors with its new ponycar stablemate, the Challenger. These included Plum Crazy, Sublime, Go-Mango, Hemi Orange and Banana; all optional. There were thirteen standard exterior colors to choose from.

The 1970 Charger had a new grille, loop front bumper and rear taillights. The R/T had a flat, reverse-facing scoop on the doors.

In all other respects, the 1970 Charger was the same car that had earned the respect of enthusiasts for the previous two years—the literal embodiment of performance and muscle car aesthetics.

Despite all this, sales plummeted. In fact, sales of practically all performance cars took a nose dive in 1970. The reason for this was the insurance industry's crackdown on insuring such cars. The surcharge on such a car as the Hemi Charger R/T would sometimes be more per year than the car payments. Consequently, sales for the Charger R/T dropped from a high of over 20,000 units in 1969 down to 10,337 in 1970. Dodge's own new Challenger was partly responsible for the drop in Charger sales.

The Charger was a popular vehicle in movies and on television. One of the most famous chase sequences appeared in *Bullitt* (1968). In this fast-paced film, Steve McQueen portrayed Frank Bullitt, an independent San Francisco cop. The chase sequence involved two hit men in a '68 Charger R/T with Bullitt driving a '68 Mustang in hot pursuit. In order for the cars to withstand the severe punishment on San Francisco's rollercoaster streets, the suspension components had to be modified. Koni shocks were installed on both cars. The Charger spring rates were increased. Many parts of both cars were magnafluxed to detect any hairline cracks which could prove fatal. The Charger was driven by stuntman Bill Hickman, who also played the role of one of the hit men. McQueen did much of the driving in the film, but the really dangerous scenes, such as the leaps, were done by Bud Ekins. The fiery crash of the Charger that climaxes the chase was accomplished by hooking up the Charger alongside the Mustang with a connecting bar and release pin pulled from the Mustang's driver seat. The Charger had rigged explosives and impact switches so it would blow up and be engulfed in flames upon hitting dummy gasoline pumps. To this day, *Bullitt* remains the standard by which all other car chase scenes are measured.

A 1970 Charger, along with its passengers, met a spectacular demise in the 1974 film, *Dirty Mary, Crazy Larry.* Peter Fonda played a racing driver and Adam Roarke his mechanic, both down on their luck and money. They resort to robbing a supermarket and spend the rest of the movie running from the law. Along the way they pick up Susan George and discard various stolen cars to avoid being spotted. They steal a 1970 Charger by driving

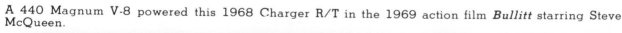

A 440 Magnum V-8 powered this 1968 Charger R/T in the 1969 action film *Bullitt* starring Steve McQueen.

it through a used-car showroom plate-glass window, and elude the police by driving into a citrus grove and getting lost in the maze. In their break toward freedom, they race for some railroad tracks. Just before they cross the tracks, a huge diesel locomotive darts in front of them, and the startling crash that follows is one of the most perfectly timed and filmed scenes ever put on film.

The most famous car in the history of television has to be the *General Lee* seen in *The Dukes of Hazzard*. The *General,* a seemingly indestructible 1969 Charger, was actually many identical cars. Whenever one car made a spectacular leap and was damaged beyond drivability, another one was waiting out of camera range.

The basic Chargers used in the series were acquired by an outside contractor through newspaper ads and word of mouth. These cars were completely refurbished with new parts from the ground up and then handed over to the studio. The studio transportation department then painted each car orange and added the Confederate flag on the roof and 01 to the doors. The engine—be it 318, 383, or 440—received a high-performance carb and aluminum intake manifold. New gas-type shock absorbers improved handling and new radial tires were fitted with inner tubes for an extra margin of safety. Because of the Charger's performance styling and its long stock car racing heritage, the car was a perfect choice for the series.

Clearly, the 1968-70 Dodge Charger was the right car at the right time. Its handsome, timeless styling would disappear in 1971, when it was completely restyled. Thus, that Charger is a prime collector car today.

In 1973, Bob McCurry of Chrysler donated a Dodge Daytona to the Daytona International Raceway museum. McCurry remarked, "The Daytona was the first car designed specifically for stock car racing . . . but its contribution to technology of aerodynamics and car design is seen in many of our current Dodge and Chrysler models. The Daytona also marks the end of an era in racing. It is a symbol of the special breed of cars which were developed when factories were active in racing."

The production Daytona also marked the apex of Dodge high-performance cars. With the mountain of government regulations looming just over the horizon and ever-changing NASCAR rules, the Daytona remains among the rarest and mightiest of Mopars.

All the Dodge Chargers used for the *General Lee* in *The Dukes of Hazzard* are carefully rebuilt. Old parts are replaced, high-performance tires and shock absorbers installed, and the car repainted as the *General Lee.* The frame of each car is weighted at four strategic points to keep it level during its unbelievable jumps. (Warner Bros Television)

CHAPTER SIX

Roots Of The Rapid Transit System 1965-1969

*"T*he Roaring '65s" is how Plymouth labeled its 1965 line of cars. The mid-size Belvedere boasted new, crisper styling, although the rooflines of the two-door and four-door models were the same as the year before. Most obvious was the switch from dual to single headlights.

There was a new model, called the Satellite. It replaced the Sport Fury as the top of the performance line, and the 119-inch-wheelbase Fury became more of a personal luxury car. The Satellite was essentially a sportier Belvedere, with the same 116-inch wheelbase and body. It was available as a two-door hardtop and convertible. The 273-ci V-8 with three-speed manual transmission was standard. It came with individual bucket seats and center console. The Satellite and Belvedere were available in fifteen standard exterior colors or fifteen optional two-tone exterior colors. A variety of cloth and vinyl interior fabrics in compatible colors was offered. Base list price for the Satellite was $3,045.

Optional engines for the Satellite and Belvedere included the 230-hp 318, the 265-hp 361 Commando, the 330-hp 383 Commando and the 365-hp 426 Commando. The 425-hp 426 Super Commando was also listed in the 1965 Plymouth brochure, but was "Not recommended for general highway driving." The 426 Super Commando wasn't covered by Plymouth's five-year or 50,000-mile engine and drivetrain warranty, due to its obvious intended purpose. The 426 race Hemi was such a rarity, it was not listed in the brochure.

To advertise the new Satellite, Plymouth chose the 426 Commando engine and used its torque reading of 470 pounds-feet at 3200 rpm as the photo caption. The first ad line read, "For a street machine, Plymouth Belvedere Satellite's acceleration curve reads like something out of a science fiction magazine."

Plymouth continued its winning ways on drag strips and circle tracks. Hemi-powered Belvederes had taken thirteen firsts out of eighteen USAC-sanctioned stock car events, to give Plymouth the undisputed Manufacturers Championship title in 1965. Norm Nelson was the top driver in USAC point standings.

Due to NASCAR's temporary ban on the 426 Hemi during half of 1965, Richard Petty wasn't able to repeat winning the Grand National title as he had in 1964.

On the strip, the Golden Commandos helped to garner twenty class wins by Plymouth at the AHRA Winter Championships at Detroit Dragway. In August, at Palmdale, California, Shirley Shahan pushed her Hemi-powered Plymouth *Drag-on-Lady* to an S/SA top speed of 129.30 mph. At the *Cars* magazine meet that month in Cecil County, Maryland, Hemi-powered Plymouths won three classes.

These were among the most notable in a long list of USAC, AHRA and NHRA wins for Plymouth in 1965, with most of the awards won by Belvederes.

For 1966, Plymouth had big news in store. The Belvedere/Satellite line was redesigned inside and out. Wheelbase remained at 116 inches. Performance styling was still not present in Plymouth's mid-size cars, but it was in the works in the styling studios.

Performance, however, was present in abundance. At the time of the introduction of Plymouth's 1966 models, the 325-hp four-barrel 383 was the most powerful V-8 you could order in your Belvedere or Satellite. The 365-hp 440-ci V-8 was introduced that year to the Plymouth line, but was available only in the full-size Fury and a new model called the VIP. The new Dodge Charger and Coronet were available with the new 426 street Hemi some months after new-year introductions, and Plymouth followed suit by making its 426 street Hemi available in the Belvedere and Satellite.

When you ordered the 425-hp dual four-barrel 426 Hemi in your Belvedere or Satellite, you got more than just the engine; you got all the hardware to back it up. This included bigger drum brakes. Front brakes were 11x3 inches and rear brakes were 11x2.5 inches, for a total of thirty-five percent more braking area than with standard brakes.

The suspension was heavy-duty all the way around. High-speed Goodyear 7.75x14 tires were mounted to wide-rim wheels.

Because of the awesome torque and horsepower of the Hemi, the three-speed manual column shift was deleted as standard equipment. You chose between the TorqueFlight automatic transmission or the four-speed manual transmission. The standard 8¾-inch, 3.23:1 rear axle was retained when the TorqueFlight was ordered, because the transmission itself served to absorb some shock of foot-to-the-floor acceleration. Included with the TorqueFlight was a small transmission fluid cooler that

The Satellite first appeared in 1965 as the top of the Plymouth Belvedere line. It was available as a two-door hardtop or convertible with bucket seats, all-vinyl trim interior and console, all standard.

prevented overheating. Overheating of the transmission fluid in Hemi-powered cars was no longer a problem due to low-speed city traffic and idling in gear.

Four-speed manual-transmission-equipped Hemi Belvederes received driveline insurance using a heavy-duty Dana Model 60 rear axle. This was really a truck axle, and could take whatever the Hemi could dish out. The axle ratio was 3.23:1.

The Sure-Grip differential was optional for both the four-speed and automatic transmissions.

Plymouths powered by the new production Hemi could be identified by a distinctive HP^2 medallion on the front fenders.

How did the 1966 Hemi-powered Satellite perform on the quarter-mile strip? One magazine achieved a 0-60 mph time of 7.4 seconds with an elapsed time of 14.5 seconds. With street tires, this was below average. Many variables entered into a Hemi Mopar's times at the drag strip. Such factors as automatic or manual transmission, standard or Sure-Grip differential and rear axle ratio affected elapsed times.

Chrysler was slugging it out with Ford on the racetrack as well as the showroom floor. It was a tumultuous year for both companies' racing efforts because NASCAR was rewriting the rule book on a monthly basis to deal with Chrysler's 426 Hemi and Ford's sohc 427. While dealing with constantly changing rules, Richard Petty won the Daytona 500, the Darlington Rebel 400, the 400-mile race in Atlanta and five other minor NASCAR races in his Hemi Belvedere. The Grand National title eluded his grasp, however.

On the USAC trail, Norm Nelson once again displayed winning form and garnered the 1966 championship by taking the checkered flag in seven of the eighteen scheduled races. He was aided by teammate Jim Hurtubise. During the summer months, both cars were emblazoned with the words Chrysler Plymouth GTX. Race fans didn't know the significance of GTX until Plymouth introduced that model in the fall of 1966.

The 426 Hemi proved to be an even more formidable engine in drag racing than previous wedge designs. Jere Stahl, of Stahl headers fame, was among the first to race a Hemi-powered Belvedere in A/Stock class; and consistently clocked elapsed times of under twelve seconds against the likes of Bill "Grumpy" Jenkins. Stahl won the Top Stock Eliminator title at the NHRA Springnationals at Bristol, Tennessee, with a time of 11.80 seconds at 119.20 mph. He then went on to cop the title again at the Sum-

The Belvedere/Satellite line was restyled for 1966. V-8's all the way up to the 426 Hemi were available.

71

mernationals at Indianapolis. Finally, Stahl took the Top Stock Eliminator crown at the NHRA World Championship Finals in Tulsa, Oklahoma, with a time of 11.65 seconds at 122.44 mph. Stahl's efforts were among the most conspicuous in a winning Mopar drag racing season.

In September 1966, Plymouth introduced its 1967 line of cars. The top of the Belvedere line was the new Belvedere GTX. This was the first mid-size Plymouth designed and sold as a performance car with a distinct identity. It was offered with a high level of trim inside and out.

The first tip-off that the GTX was a muscle car to be reckoned with was the two nonfunctional hood scoops. There was a pit-stop-style gas cap on the left rear fender. GTX medallions were affixed to the front fenders and there was one on the right side of the trunk lid. Chromed dual exhaust outlets finished off the rear end appearance of the GTX.

Inside, the GTX featured saddle-grain vinyl with luxurious "tooled leather" design on the front and rear seats. The center console separating the front bucket seats came with side-mounted courtesy lights and lockable storage compartment. The rear seats were specially padded to simulate bucket seats. At no extra cost, you could delete the standard console and order a combination armrest and center seat to allow room for three up front.

The GTX was powered by the new 375-hp 440 Super Commando four-barrel V-8. It was backed up by a rugged TorqueFlight automatic transmission. The four-speed manual transmission was optional as part of the Special Performance Package, which included a Sure-Grip differential ratio of 3.55:1. The 426 Hemi was optional. The standard rear axle ratio was 3.23:1, but a 2.93:1 ratio was optional.

The suspension was heavy-duty. Included were heavy-duty torsion bars, front antisway bar, parallel asymmetrical rear leaf springs that were beefed up to counteract torque-steer and control rear wheel hop, heavy-duty Oriflow shocks, Red Streak tires mounted on 14x5.5K wide-rim wheels, and 11x3-inch front and 11x2½-inch rear heavy-duty drum brakes. If you ordered a Satellite or Belvedere with the 426 Hemi, you got this heavy-duty suspension as part of the Hemi option. Practically all GTX's were photographed with the handsome chrome custom road wheels and dual sport stripes on the hood and trunk, but these were optional, not standard.

The 1967 Satellite had Aluma-Plate finish running the length of the lower body. This one is powered by the 426 Hemi.

The base list price for the GTX hardtop was $3,330. Plymouth sold 12,690 of them in 1967.

The 1967 GTX was capable of reaching 60 mph in seven seconds and covering the quarter mile in 14.4 seconds.

The appearance of the Belvedere and Satellite was altered slightly by the switch from two to four headlights in 1967. Also, Satellites that year featured a special satin-silver Aluma-Plate finish on the full length of the lower body; this was absent on the GTX. The Satellite interior, however, was shared by the GTX.

A brochure for the 1967 line of Belvederes stated that the top engine available in the Satellite and Belvedere was the 325-hp four-barrel 383 V-8, and the 426 Hemi was optional only in the GTX. Plymouth must have changed its mind, because Satellites were photographed with the 426 Hemi medallion, now located on the front fender just above the rocker panel.

All GTX, Satellite and Belvedere convertibles now had a glass back window instead of plastic. There were nineteen exterior paint colors to choose from.

According to *Car Craft* magazine, 1967 Belvederes were also available in what Plymouth called A/Stock trim. Sound deadener and insulation were not installed on these cars, the battery was mounted in the trunk for better weight distribution, a functional hood scoop was installed and the 426 street Hemi was the powerplant. These limited production Belvederes were lighter and less expensive than the GTX and made drag racing more affordable for neophytes. They were the ultimate "trick" Mopars on the street that year, also.

NASCAR finally stopped playing its shell game with engine displacement rules, and the 426 Hemi was given the green light during the latter part of 1966. Thirty-year-old Richard Petty was thus ready to dominate stock car racing with his #43 blue Hemi-powered GTX. He entered forty-eight Grand National races that year and won an unprecedented twenty-seven races. Once again, Petty walked away with the Grand National title, and a total of $130,275 in prize money.

Plymouth did not win the manufacturers title on the USAC circuit in 1967. That honor went to Dodge and its driver Don White.

The 1967 GTX was Plymouth's first high-visibility super car. It was available as a two-door hardtop or convertible.

Ronnie Sox and Buddy Martin were emerging in the late sixties as one of the most popular and successful drag racing partnerships. They chose Plymouth, and their distinctive red, white and blue cars became their trademark. In 1967, they campaigned a Hemi-powered Belvedere GTX in the stock classes. Their most notable win that year was at the NHRA Springnationals in Bristol, Tennessee, where they handily won S/S class.

Drag racer Don Grotheer was also a Plymouth man. He raced his 1967 Super Stocker on the NHRA circuit. At the Winternationals at Pomona, California, Grotheer was AA/S class winner. He went on to become the NHRA Division 4 Super Stock Eliminator points winner.

The Belvedere line was completely restyled for 1968. Distinctive styling touches were the long creases on the sides of the front and rear fenders and the unique "ribbon" rear window. Front amber and rear red side-marker lights were a new safety feature. Wheelbase remained at 116 inches. Front and rear tracks were increased roughly one-half inch.

It was also a very good year for Plymouth performance cars. One of the most famous muscle cars in history was introduced in 1968—the Road Runner. Joe Sturm was a Plymouth product planner at the time. Sturm made a presentation to the Detroit Chapter of the Society of Automotive Engineers in September 1969, telling how the Road Runner was born.

In the early months of 1967, Sturm received a call from the sales division asking him, "Why not offer a car that has the biggest engine we make as standard equipment. A car that has no rear seats, no floor mats and eliminate every piece of trim and ornamentation?" The concept for the vehicle was obviously race car inspired.

Sturm discussed the idea with Jack Smith and Gordon Cherry and they agreed that this kind of stripped car would appeal to too small a group of buyers. However, they felt there was a significant market for a relatively inexpensive car deliberately devoid of interior and exterior frills, with maximum attention to engine, driveline, suspension and brakes.

In order to substantiate the concept and properly target the car, an in-depth look at the high-performance market—both cars and buyers—

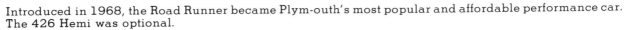
Introduced in 1968, the Road Runner became Plym-outh's most popular and affordable performance car. The 426 Hemi was optional.

was conducted. The study revealed five distinct levels of knowledge and interest in cars by enthusiasts, forming a pyramid according to the size of each group.

At the top were the elite professional racers. Sturm said, "While this group is small, they exert the greatest degree of influence on the group. Their opinions and actions serve to direct and mold the desires and attitudes of the balance of the enthusiast market."

Next came the hard-core, but not professional, racers, who regard the appearance and reputation of a car of lesser importance than ultimate top speed.

The third group consisted of part-time enthusiasts and racers, who have a dual-purpose machine—one that is driven on the street and strip. This group put a greater importance on a car's appearance.

The fourth group, which Sturm called the "executive hot rodders," like high performance but place the most importance on a good-looking machine.

The plush interior of the 1968 GTX came from the Satellite. Bucket seats and console were standard.

The 1968 GTX came standard with a 375-hp four-barrel 440 V-8. It was available as a hardtop or convertible. This one had the optional chrome-plated steel road wheels.

The last and largest group was the "Drive-In Set"—the street cruisers, spectators and identifiers who are into performance. The members of this group devour the performance buff magazines for the latest low-buck hop-up tricks because they have the least amount of money of the five groups. However, because of its size, it buys the most cars. This last group was the target group for the car Plymouth had in mind.

Plymouth also studied the high-performance cars on the market. "In order to determine what performance level was necessary for this proposed car and what price tag the car could support," said Sturm, "the existing offerings of that time were reviewed in detail." A chart was made giving quarter-mile trap speed vertically on the left, and price increasing from left to right. Not surprisingly, he found the more you spent, the faster you went. A cluster of cars priced over $3,300 was capable of over 100 mph in the quarter mile, but there wasn't one car on the market below $3,300 with the same performance.

With this information, Plymouth's initial goal was to build a car capable of 100 mph in the quarter mile with a retail price of $3,000. "To accomplish this," Sturm said, "it was necessary to eliminate some of the more costly appointments that characterized the earlier kinds of super cars. The expense of the extra brightwork and high interior trim level was converted to the performance engine and chassis hardware."

At the top of the list of standard equipment was a modified four-barrel 383 V-8 with the cylinder heads, intake manifold, exhaust manifolds, crankcase windage tray, camshaft and valve springs used in the 375-hp high-performance 440 V-8. An unsilenced air cleaner helped boost power by a few horsepower and increased induction roar. This engine, rated at 335 hp, was available only in the Road Runner and no other Plymouth. However, the Dodge equivalent of this engine was available in the Coronet Super Bee. The 426 Hemi was optional in the Road Runner for $714.30.

A four-speed manual transmission was standard and used fine-pitch gears. When the Hemi was ordered, the transmission came with coarse-pitch gears, with bushings between the shafts and gears, along with a larger input shaft. Both transmissions had the same ratios.

The Air Grabber cool-air induction system was introduced during 1968 on the Road Runner and GTX.

There were two optional TorqueFlight automatic transmissions, depending on which engine was used. The transmission ordered on the 383 V-8 had four discs and a two-inch kickdown band. The transmission ordered with the Hemi used five discs and a 2½-inch kickdown band. Both automatic transmissions were designed for high-competition upshifts with high-stall-speed converters. These TorqueFlights cost only $38.95, and they were practically bulletproof for the drag strip.

The standard heavy-duty suspension used all the usual parts based on previous Belvedere experience. If the Hemi was ordered, the front torsion bars were beefed up to handle the Hemi's extra weight, and the number of rear spring leaves increased from 4½ to six on the left and 6½ on the right. This was necessary to prevent torque steer. Chrysler found that if you floored the Hemi Road Runner with just the heavy-duty suspension, the car would actually jump to the right an entire lane! Chrysler first discovered this characteristic in 1963 Max Wedge-powered cars and beefed up the rear suspension to cure it. Subsequent big-block Mopars got the same treatment.

Eleven-inch heavy-duty drum brakes were standard, but optional front disc brakes could be ordered for $72.95.

The F70x14 Red Streak Wide Boot tires were standard. F70x14 White Streak Wide Boot tires were a no-cost option. When you ordered the Hemi, F70x15 Red Streak Wide Boot tires were standard.

You could dress up your Road Runner a bit with the Custom Styled road wheel for $97.30.

The standard rear axle ratio was 3.23:1, but there were several options. It cost $42.35 to get the 3.23:1 axle with Sure-Grip. A High-Performance Axle Package included a heavy-duty 3.55:1 Sure-Grip ratio, slip-drive fan, a wider heavy-duty radiator and a fan shroud for $87.50. When you ordered a Hemi with the four-speed manual transmission, a heavy-duty 3.54 Sure-Grip Dana 60 differential was a mandatory option costing $138.90.

The interior was spartan, to keep the cost down. A bench seat was used instead of front bucket seats. Three interior color combinations were

The 1968 Road Runner came with its own special engine, a four-barrel 383 with 335 hp. Note the air cleaner decal.

available: two-tone blue, parchment and tan, and silver and black. The carpeted floor was black. A Custom Decor Package for $79.20 expanded the choice of colors to eight, and included a special steering wheel with partial horn ring, a bright outside cap on the center pillar, and a custom appliqué on the deck lid coordinated with the taillights.

The most distinguishing appearance feature of the Road Runner was the standard performance hood. The two-foot-long, side-facing integral hood scoops were nonfunctional at first. The engine displacement was displayed on the inside of the die-cast pieces. When the Hemi was ordered, the word Hemi appeared on the scoops and on the rear of the car.

A mid-year option on the 1968 Road Runner made the hood scoops functional. A knob beneath the dash controlled flaps inside the underhood ductwork running from the scoops to the engine air cleaner. In the closed position, holes in the bottom of the ductwork permitted only underhood air to get to the engine, to speed warm-up. By pulling the knob underneath the dash, the flaps inside the ductwork covered the holes and opened the ductwork to permit cool outside air to enter the scoops. This did not offer a dramatic increase in power, but it was a tremendous image builder.

A matte-black performance hood patch for $17.55 drew attention to the hood scoops, and many Road Runners were ordered with it.

Just how did the Road Runner get its name? A long list of names was studied. "The name Road Runner had shown up on lists off and on for a couple of years," recalled Sturm, "but apparently neither the product was right, nor had the correct 'sell' job been done to get it considered. Jack Smith and Gordon Cherry, the top two Belvedere product planners at the time, sent me home to watch the Saturday Road Runner cartoon show." After watching the show, Sturm agreed that Road Runner was a perfect

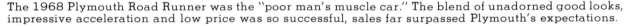

The 1968 Plymouth Road Runner was the "poor man's muscle car." The blend of unadorned good looks, impressive acceleration and low price was so successful, sales far surpassed Plymouth's expectations.

name for this new performance car. The whimsical cartoon character's traits of almost unlimited speed and unperturbed stopping power made the name an ideal choice.

"We were amazed to find that we could put a hold on the name Road Runner for a car at the AMA [Automotive Manufacturers Association]," Sturm added. "That started the process which eventually led to the Plymouth Division adopting the name Road Runner for the new car. Subsequently, agreement was reached with Warner Bros. to use their particular copyrighted cartoon character instead of our own, which we had under development."

Plymouth planners didn't stop at the name. They pulled a marketing coup that gladdened the sales division's heart. The product planners actually duplicated the two-legged Road Runner's "Beep-Beep" by having their horn vendor use copper windings instead of the usual aluminum. The horn was so accurate that only a trained technician could tell the difference.

Finally, a Road Runner nameplate appeared on the dash, on the trunk lid and on the doors, along with a small cartoon of the speedy bird.

As set up within the cost parameters, Plymouth's drag strip tests of the car produced a trap speed of 98 mph. This was slightly below expectations, but it was still faster than anything else at the same price.

Young performance-minded buyers agreed. Plymouth's sales and marketing people thought only 2,500 Road Runners would be sold its first year. They were astounded when 45,000 were sold. The Road Runner was a hit!

If any car could steal the attention from the Road Runner at the local burger drive-in, it was the 1968 GTX. The GTX had become a popular choice with amateur and professional drag racers because of its standard 375-hp 440 in 1967. Its reputation as a winner in the quarter mile soon earned it the label "the boss."

For 1968, the boss was back with handsome new Belvedere Satellite sheetmetal. And it shared the same performance hood with the Road Runner. Displacement was shown in the center of the hood scoops.

GTX medallions appeared in the center of the front grille, on the lower rear fenders just before the wheelwell, and in the center of the full-width die-cast trim plate across the rear deck. There were dual lower body accent stripes in a choice of five colors. The rocker panels were set off with a polished aluminum trim strip.

The overall appearance of the GTX made it apparent this was the top of the Belvedere line. Tasteful brightwork accented the car inside and out. The interior was redesigned but retained the standard front bucket seats with center console. Door and instrument panels were trimmed with simulated walnut grain. Seat belts were standard. There were eight interior colors available.

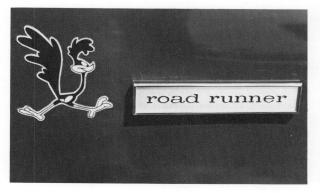

This final design for the Road Runner cartoon figure and medallion was approved for 1968 production.

The GTX was again available as a two-door hardtop or convertible. The convertible had a glass rear window. Because of the inherently clean lines of the Belvedere, the 1968 GTX convertible was, and still is, one of the finest statements of top-down, high-performance driving to come from Plymouth, or anybody else for that matter.

Streetwise kids knew GTX meant 440 cubic inches under the hood. The 426 Hemi was optional. The TorqueFlight automatic transmission was again standard, but the four-speed manual transmission was optional at no extra cost. When the four-speed was ordered, it came with the Performance Package that included the heavy-duty Dana 60 rear axle with a 3.54:1 Sure-Grip ratio.

Production for the 1968 GTX totaled 18,940.

Car Life magazine was a popular performance enthusiast magazine during the sixties. The performance findings at the drag strip for the 1968 Road Runner and GTX were interesting. The Road Runner, with automatic transmission, did 0-60 mph in 7.3 seconds. It covered the quarter mile in 15.4 seconds, but trap speed was only 91 mph. The four-speed manual transmission offered a dramatic improvement over this. Top speed for the Road Runner was 122 mph.

The GTX with standard 440 V-8 and automatic transmission, did 0-60 mph in 6.8 seconds. It reached the quarter-mile timing lights in 14.6 seconds at 96 mph. Top speed was 121 mph.

Car Life naturally found the Hemi-powered GTX one of the fastest cars it ever tested. Even with an automatic transmission, the Hemi GTX reached 60 mph in 6.3 seconds. The quarter mile was covered in 14.0 seconds at 97 mph. Top speed was an astounding 144 mph.

Despite the smoother Belvedere shape for 1968, Plymouth did not fare well on the NASCAR circuit that year. Ford had introduced the fastback Torino, and Mercury had a fastback called the Cyclone. Plymouth's ace-in-the-hole, Richard Petty, was just not able to keep up. The Belvedere's aerodynamic disadvantage would force Petty to switch to Ford for the 1969 racing season.

The USAC story for 1968 was much the same. Ford cleaned up here, followed by Dodge.

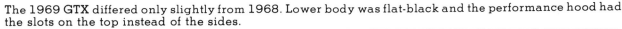
The 1969 GTX differed only slightly from 1968. Lower body was flat-black and the performance hood had the slots on the top instead of the sides.

The Road Runner and GTX found better luck on the drag strips. These high-visibility cars were becoming increasingly popular with drag racing fans, and they had the power under the hood to win. Again, the team of Sox & Martin was the most conspicuous in racing Plymouths. For 1968 they chose a Street Hemi Road Runner for Super Stock class racing. Against extremely tough competition (Chevys, Fords and Dodges were neck and neck in the horsepower race), Sox & Martin garnered one NHRA and three AHRA titles that year.

When they weren't racing successfully, Ronnie Sox and Buddy Martin conducted the Plymouth SuperCar Clinics. These seminars were held at Plymouth dealerships around the country to give Plymouth fans drag racing and car preparation tips. In the larger cities, sometimes over 2,000 people would attend.

If 1968 was a good year for Plymouth fans, 1969 was even better. The Road Runner coupe was joined by two new models: a pillarless hardtop and a convertible. All three Road Runner models had a new front grille and rear taillights. The performance hood scoops now were open on the top instead of the sides.

In the 1969 Belvedere brochure, Plymouth formally announced the optional Air Grabber, making the hood scoops functional. The Air Grabber ductwork was made of fiberglass and bolted to the underside of the hood. It was painted a bright red orange and an Air Grabber decal was affixed to it. The ductwork straddled a large oval air cleaner as the hood was closed. Rubber seals between the ductwork and the air cleaner ensured proper performance.

The Air Grabber was optional in the Road Runner with the standard 335-hp 383 V-8. (The Road Runner 383 V-8 was now painted a Hemi orange.) It was optional in the Belvedere and Satellite with the optional 330-hp Super Commando 383, but was standard when the Hemi was ordered in the Road Runner or GTX. Cost of the Air Grabber alone was $55.30. The 426 Hemi option cost $813.45 in the Road Runner, and $700.90 in the GTX.

The Road Runner was offered in eighteen exterior colors, with eight interior colors for the coupe and hardtop, and six interior colors for the convertible. Bucket seats were a new option.

There was a larger color cartoon of the Road Runner on the deck lid, doors and instrument panel, and one now also appeared on the steering wheel hub.

The air-control doors in the 1969 Air Grabber performance hood permitted either cool outside air or warm underhood air to feed the engine. The inlets were moved from the side of the scoops to the top in 1969.

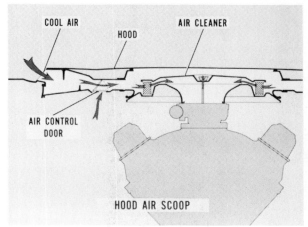

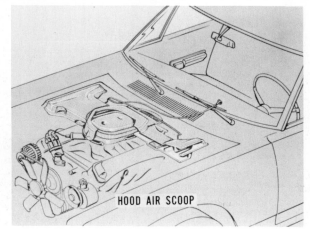

When intrigued bystanders had asked to see the famous "Beep-Beep" horn under the hood of the 1968 Road Runner, they had been disappointed to find a simple black device. For 1969, the horn was painted a light purple and a decal was affixed to it that read, "The Voice of the Road Runner."

Changes to the 1969 GTX were also subtle. The front grille was different, with a two-bar motif in red with GTX mounted in the center. The

For 1969, Plymouth called its cool-air induction system, optional on the Road Runner four-barrel 383 V-8, the Coyote Duster.

The 1969 440 6-bbl Road Runner was an ideal street/strip car for young enthusiasts. The huge fiberglass hood offered better performance than the Air Grabber induction system. The fiberglass hood could quickly be removed and placed on the car's roof.

taillights were recessed. The polished aluminum trim strips on the lower body were replaced by a flat-black paint treatment with a thin red or white reflective stripe. As on all Belvedere models, the side-marker lights were now rectangular instead of round. The seat facings in the GTX were new, and the interior was available in eleven colors. The GTX was available in eighteen exterior colors.

The standard performance specifications of both the 1969 Road Runner and GTX remained unchanged from 1968. However, there were numerous new options that could boost the performance of these cars.

At the top of the list was, of course, the 426 Hemi, which came standard with the Air Grabber.

The really big news for performance buffs in 1969 was the wide selection of higher numerical rear axle ratios and related equipment.

The Performance Axle Package included a 3.55:1 axle ratio with Sure-Grip differential. A viscous drive fan with fan shrouds and extra-wide twenty-six-inch radiator helped keep the engine cool during racing. A Road Runner Hemi suspension was also included, but this was standard on the GTX.

The High-Performance Axle Package included all the equipment from the Performance Axle Package but used a 3.91:1 axle ratio. This package was available only in the Road Runner and other Belvederes or Satellites with four-barrel 383 V-8 engines.

The Super-Performance Axle Package had all the equipment from the Performance Axle Package, with 4.10:1 axle ratio instead. This was available only with the four-barrel 440 V-8 and 426 Hemi with TorqueFlight automatic transmission.

The Trak Pak included a Hurst four-speed shifter, extra-heavy-duty Dana 60 3.54:1 rear axle with Sure-Grip differential, viscous drive fan and

Minor changes to the 1969 Road Runner were primarily limited to appearance. Sales of the 1969 Road Runner doubled from 1968.

dual-breaker distributor. The Trak Pak was available only on the GTX and Hemi-powered Plymouths.

Finally, the Super Trak Pak included all the items in the Trak Pak but substituted a 4.10:1 axle ratio and included power front disc brakes. The Super Trak Pak was available only on the GTX and Hemi-powered Plymouths.

There were also new performance appearance options to distinguish your mighty Mopar in 1969. To set off the performance hood of your Road Runner or GTX, you could order the new optional performance hood treatment with two broad bands of flat-black paint that ran from the windshield to the grille. The centers of the hood scoops were painted red for a dramatic effect.

Besides the handsome five-spoke steel road wheel, there was a new cast aluminum-construction five-slot road wheel pictured in the 1969 Belvedere brochure.

A manually adjusted driver seat moved fore and aft and up and down, and tilted, giving 160 different positions. The center console, once standard in the GTX, was now optional in the GTX, as well as the Road Runner and Sport Satellite. An 8000 rpm tachometer was still an option in the GTX and Road Runner.

You could order power windows, power front disc brakes, power steering and a host of other options to make driving your GTX or Road Runner more enjoyable. If you wanted air conditioning, though, you couldn't order the 426 Hemi or Air Grabber option.

The dust had hardly settled around the introduction of the 1969 Road Runner when *Motor Trend* gave it the Car of the Year award. In conjunction with and to commemorate this award, Plymouth introduced a new Road Runner in the spring of 1969. This Road Runner was called, simply, 440 6-bbl.

The 440 6-bbl Road Runner was available as a hardtop or coupe, but not as a convertible. It was powered by a specially modified 440-ci Super

The Road Runner convertible was introduced in 1969 and built that year only. It is one of the rarest of Road Runners and those still existing command hefty price tags among collectors.

Commando engine with three Holley two-barrel carburetors on an Edelbrock aluminum intake manifold. This engine churned out 390 hp with 490 pounds-feet of torque at 3600 rpm.

As on all Road Runners, a four-speed manual transmission and Hurst shifter were standard, as were eleven-inch heavy-duty drum brakes. A maximum-capacity cooling system was also standard. A 4.10:1 Sure-Grip differential was part of the package. The car rode on Goodyear G70x15 Red Streak tires mounted on 15x6-inch wheels painted black, with chrome lug nuts.

The 440 6-bbl Road Runner could easily be identified by its fiberglass hood with huge functional scoop. A 440 6-bbl decal appeared on the sides of the scoop. The hood was finished in a special flat-black paint with four chrome locking pins to secure the hood, similar to the way the hood operated on the Super Stock Hemi Barracuda drag cars. The four pins were removed and the hood could be placed on the roof when the engine was serviced.

The car was offered in four brilliant colors—Performance Red, Bahama Yellow, Rallye Green, Vitamin C Orange—and white.

The best news of all to Mopar performance buffs was the price—$462.80 over the base Road Runner. The 440 6-bbl Road Runner was cheaper to buy and maintain than a Hemi Road Runner and—if Plymouth's own ads were to be believed—faster in the quarter mile. Roland McGonegal, with *Super Stock* magazine, averaged a 13.50-second elapsed time at 109.31 mph. Chrysler's own Dick Maxwell averaged 13.59 seconds at 105.63 mph in a Hemi Road Runner.

With performance like this, it's no wonder the Road Runner was one of the hottest-selling performance cars in 1969. Sales nearly doubled in 1969 to 85,000 units. No doubt the Road Runner lured away some prospective GTX buyers; sales of the GTX dropped from 18,940 in 1968 to 15,608 in 1969.

With Richard Petty racing a Ford in 1969, Plymouth won only two Grand National stock car races. Ford won twenty-six races and Dodge won twenty-two. However, Roger McCluskey won the 1969 USAC championship racing a Plymouth Road Runner. Sox & Martin switched to a Barracuda for drag racing activities in 1969, so most of the wins by Belvedere Road Runners and GTX's were at the hands of lesser known professionals and amateurs.

Plymouth finished its B-body muscle car efforts in the sixties with a bang. The show would prove tough to top in the seventies.

Roger McCluskey won the 1969 USAC stock car title in a Hemi-powered Road Runner.

CHAPTER SEVEN

From Coronet To Super Bee Six-Pack 1965-1970

Dodge introduced the Coronet in 1965. This was a new model in the intermediate-size field. The Coronet would be the basis of Dodge's performance efforts for the rest of the sixties. In 1965, however, the Coronet did not have a performance model per se, like Pontiac's GTO. Nevertheless, you could order horsepower in abundance.

The 1965 Coronet had a 117-inch wheelbase, one inch longer than the 1964 Dodge. The roofline was borrowed from the previous year, but the entire body differed completely for the 1965 Dodge. The car featured four headlights instead of two.

The Coronet was offered in four series: Coronet, Coronet Deluxe, 440 and 500. A total of seventeen different models was available, which included two-door and four-door hardtops, two-door and four-door sedans, two-door convertibles, and station wagons.

The Coronet 500 was the dressiest model. It was equivalent to Plymouth's Satellite, and comparably equipped. The standard interior featured front bucket seats and center console.

When it came to engines, freedom of choice was the norm in the sixties, unlike today. The 225-ci one-barrel six was standard in the base Coronet, along with a three-speed column-mounted manual transmission. There were many optional V-8's advertised, and one V-8 available that few knew about. The smallest V-8 was the 180-hp two-barrel 273. Next was the 230-hp two-barrel 318. More power could be had from the 361-ci two-barrel V-8 with 265 hp. Even better was the 330-hp four-barrel 383. The top performance engine described in the 1965 Coronet brochure was the 365-hp four-barrel 426 street wedge.

How did the 365-hp street wedge 426 Coronet stack up against its competition at Ford and GM? *Motor Trend* tested a Coronet 500 with this engine and the four-speed manual transmission. It did 0-60 mph in 7.7 seconds, the quarter mile in 15.7 seconds at 89 mph, and had a top speed of 118 mph.

Although Dodge wouldn't announce the availability of the 426 street Hemi until the 1966 model year, it did advertise the availability of the race Hemi in the 1965 Coronet. The ad appeared in the December 1964 *Hot Rod,* with the tag line, "Our new 426 Coronet ought to have its head examined." The ad left no doubt the Hemi was available in the Coronet, at one point asking, "Why not drop a Hemi in the new Coronet 500?" Clearly, the implication was you could drive a Hemi Coronet on the street, but the ad failed to tell you one thing: This was a race Hemi, and ran with a 12.5:1 compression ratio. Unless you had access to racing gas or aviation fuel, driving this car on the street was highly impractical. It made far more sense to put the Hemi Coronet to its intended use on the drag strip.

Dodge strongly backed its own drag strip efforts, and continued to sell specially manufactured cars strictly for the quarter mile.

Dodge's aluminum-paneled cars were so successful on the drag strips in 1964, the NHRA revised its Super Stock rules to require cars in this class to run all-steel bodies. These cars also had to weigh at least 3,400 pounds.

Dodge honored these rules, but still came up with a car that was fast, by selling the Coronet two-door sedan with a wheelbase shortened to 115 inches. This was achieved by moving the rear wheels forward two inches. The purpose in doing this was to transfer more weight to the rear wheels and thus provide greater traction off the line.

To further reduce the weight on the front wheels, and achieve an ideal 50/50 weight balance, other measures were taken. The four-headlight grille was replaced by one using only two headlights. The front K-member was redesigned, shedding twenty-five pounds. The 426 Hemi engine was improved by the use of numerous aluminum and magnesium parts which cut nearly ninety pounds from the engine. The transmission was either the new TorqueFlight with column shift selector (the push-button Torque-Flight was no longer available) or the floor-mounted four-speed manual transmission. The 1965 Super Stock Drag Coronet was continuing evidence that Dodge was seriously committed to promoting drag racing, and drawing attention to its production cars by doing so.

The Dodge Coronet was introduced in 1965. Seventeen models were offered, including convertibles.

If more proof was needed, you only had to look at the even wilder Coronet Dodge built to compete in the A/FX (factory experimental) class. This car had an altered wheelbase of 110 inches with both front and rear wheels moved forward dramatically. In addition, the front fenders, bumper, hood with air scoop, doors, dash and rear deck lid were made of fiberglass. The Hemi engine and transmission had the same specifications as the Super Stock Coronet.

Coronets had a pretty good showing in sanctioned drag racing in 1965. At the AHRA Winter Championships in Phoenix, Arizona, Mike Buckel in the Ramchargers Coronet took Top Stock Eliminator. Buc Faubel took the Mr. Stock Eliminator class, also in a 1965 Coronet. At the NHRA Nationals at International Raceway Park in September of 1965, Bob Harrop took the S/SA class honors in a Coronet.

The 1965 NASCAR season was a fiasco for Chrysler in general and Dodge in particular. Bill France, Sr., the father of NASCAR, banned the 426 Hemi for half of 1965. This allowed Ford to walk away with numerous wins using its sohc 427. Ford won so many races that a Ford win became a foregone conclusion, and attendance dropped. Finally, Bill France permitted Hemis to race, but only in 119-inch-wheelbase cars, on tracks over one mile. On shorter tracks, the Hemi could be used in the Plymouth Belvedere and Dodge Coronet. Consequently, Hemi Coronets never saw Daytona, Talladega and the other prestigious super speedway races in 1965.

For the street Hemi, 1966 was the official year of introduction. With a compression ratio reduced to 10.5:1, altered camshaft lift and timing and other modifications, the most powerful production passenger-car engine ever built was tractable for the street. The 425-hp dual four-barrel 426 Hemi was available in the Coronet, Coronet Deluxe, Coronet 440 and Coronet 500. (The numbers 440 and 500 used in conjunction with Coronet had no significance related to either standard or optional engines. They were simply model numbers. This was true of many Dodge and Plymouth cars during the sixties.)

The Coronet was restyled for 1966. It retained the 117-inch wheelbase. Overall length was reduced from 204 inches to 203 inches. The new

The 1965 Coronet came standard with these inviting bucket seats and a center console.

lines of the Coronet were more defined and crisp. The roofline still borrowed from the past, but the entire car was fresh in appearance. Car buyers in the sixties always looked for new styling each year, either major or minor. If styling wasn't new, then some other aspect of the car, such as a new engine, had to catch the new-car buyer's attention. In 1966, everything was new about the Coronet.

The interior of the Coronet was all-new for 1966. The top-of-the-line Coronet 500 shared the same seats with the new Charger, but the Coronet did not have the Charger's space-age dash; the Coronet dash was much more conventional.

The Coronet was available in over fifteen exterior acrylic enamel colors in 1966. Interior vinyl and vinyl-with-fabric colors weren't so plentiful, but were designed to coordinate with paint color.

Standard and optional engines and transmissions remained essentially unchanged. Of course, the dual four-barrel 426 Hemi, conservatively rated at 425 hp, was the biggest news to come along in years. If you ordered a Hemi in your Coronet that year, you certainly had a sleeper on your hands. Short of popping the hood, there was little to tell the poor guy waiting in the next lane at the stoplight that you had a Hemi. This would change in the late sixties with the advent of hood scoops, racing stripes and billboard-size graphics that could be seen a block away!

How did the 1966 Hemi-powered Coronet perform? One magazine tested a Coronet 440 two-door convertible with the elephant motor and achieved 0-60 mph in 6.1 seconds, and a quarter-mile time of 14.5 seconds.

On the racetrack, it was a time of change for the two-year-old Coronet. The fastback Charger, based on the Coronet, was quickly becoming the choice of Dodge-backed drivers in NASCAR and USAC events. Despite the new Hemi, few Coronets broke into the top ranks of NHRA and AHRA Super Stock and A/Stock Automatic classes, where Plymouths were taking the lion's share of wins.

For 1967, the Coronet featured some mild facelifting in the front grille and rear taillight areas. The tapered rear roof pillar motif persisted on the two-door hardtop models. Simulated vents appeared on the sides of the Coronet 440 and 500 models, just behind the doors. The Coronet 500 received a black accent stripe along the lower beltline running the entire length of the car.

The Dodge Rebellion got a new member in 1967: the Coronet R/T. R/T stood for Road/Track, and many R/T's became dual-purpose ma-

The Coronet was restyled in 1966. The strongest engine available was the 425-hp 426 Hemi.

chines. This car's appearance differed from other Coronets by having a unique grille that resembled that of the Charger, but with exposed instead of retractable headlights. R/T badges appeared on the front grille, on the sides just behind the simulated scoops, and near the right rear taillight assembly. Nonfunctional air scoops on the hood also marked the car as an R/T. Upper and lower body side paint stripes in white, black, red or blue set off the R/T, but you could delete these on the order form.

The Coronet R/T became a dual-purpose machine for one simple reason. An ad for the car made it clear: "Enter the Big Bore Hunter," read the double-page ads in the enthusiast magazines in November 1966. Enter the 440 Magnum four-barrel V-8. This brute of an engine, with 375 hp and 480 pounds-feet of torque, was really what the R/T was all about. Essentially, this was the same engine used in Plymouth's Belvedere GTX.

The R/T, available as a two-door hardtop or convertible, was equipped to handle all that power. Heavy-duty front and rear suspension, front antisway bar, three-inch-wide heavy-duty drum brakes (front disc brakes were optional), heavy-duty shock absorbers and 7.75x14 Goodyear Red Streak tires rounded out the standard package. Base list price was $3,352.

Backing up the 440 Magnum was either the four-speed manual transmission or TorqueFlight automatic transmission as standard equipment. The 426 Hemi was optional.

Options you could order on your R/T were a Sure-Grip differential, center console, console-mounted tachometer, three-spoke simulated wood-grain steering wheel with full horn ring, mag-type wheelcovers, chromed steel road wheels, black or white Levant-grain vinyl roof, power brakes, power steering, power windows and a long list of other appearance, comfort and convenience options. Practically all these options were available on the other Coronets.

Dodge ran several different ads for the 1967 Coronet R/T. In the April 1967 issue of *Car and Driver* there appeared a very curious ad. A photomontage of the car and its specific features was set off by two bold words in lower-case letters: road runner. How could these words appear in a Dodge ad only months before Plymouth announced its Belvedere Road Runner? Certainly, it was no secret among Chrysler product planners and management that a car called the Road Runner was in the works at Plymouth. Consequently, it is odd that Dodge would take the liberty of using the words, even though the division didn't use the term as a vehicle name.

The interior of the 1966 Coronet 500 matched that of the 1966 Charger except for the rear portion of the console.

How did the Coronet R/T stack up against the Hemi-powered Coronet of the year before? The Coronet R/T reached 60 mph in 7.2 seconds and covered the quarter mile in the fourteen-second range.

Coronet R/T sales in 1967 totaled 10,109 units.

Coronet R/T's got a great deal of exposure on the drag strip thanks to drag racer Dick Landy. Landy had proved himself to be a winning driver behind the wheel of a Dodge on drag strips in the early sixties. With Dodge backing, Landy raced two R/T's, one with the standard 440 Magnum and the other with the 426 Hemi. He raced them in Super Stock class. Like Plymouth's sponsored team of Sox & Martin, Landy also conducted SuperCar Clinics at Dodge dealerships around the country.

On the NASCAR and USAC tracks, Dodge drivers had pretty much deserted the Coronet for the fastback Charger, and this would remain the case into the seventies.

Dodge announced the Scat Pack in 1968. This was a fleet of high-performance Dodge cars based on the Charger, the Coronet and the Dart. These three cars were the Charger R/T, the Coronet R/T and the Dart GTS. The cars of the Scat Pack were identified as "The Cars with the Bumblebee Stripes." These stripes were appropriately wrapped around the tail end of the cars. And it wasn't long before a fourth member joined the Scat Pack.

When Plymouth announced its low-buck street/strip racer, the Belvedere Road Runner, in 1968, Dodge did not sit idly by. The division had been preparing its own version, using the Coronet, with a name inspired by the Scat Pack bumblebee logo. It was the Coronet Super Bee.

The mid-size Coronet was a good basis for the Super Bee because it was completely restyled for 1968. The new Coronet no longer shared sheetmetal with the Charger, which was also restyled for 1968. There was, however, a family resemblance between the Coronet and Charger. Wheelbase for the Coronet remained at 117 inches, but overall length grew to 206.6 inches.

The Super Bee began life as a Coronet 440 two-door coupe. Like the Road Runner, it achieved a low price tag by deleting certain nonessential items. Roll-down rear windows were nixed in favor of more economical pop-out windows, which necessitated the use of a center pillar. It came

The Coronet Super Bee of 1968 was Dodge's equivalent to the Plymouth Road Runner. Both cars used the same 335-hp four-barrel 383 V-8, only having different names. The 426 Hemi was optional.

without a vinyl roof. The interior was the base version with a bench-type front seat. Interior and exterior trim were minimal.

Standard on the Super Bee was a 335-hp version of the four-barrel 383 V-8. The high-performance dual exhaust system had 2¼-inch exhaust pipes and tuned mufflers, with 2¼-inch tail pipes. The standard transmission was a heavy-duty four-speed manual with Hurst Competition-Plus floor shift. The shifter came with a simulated wood-grain knob and reverse-engagement warning light. The TorqueFlight automatic transmission was optional for less than fifty dollars. A heavy-duty driveshaft, rear axle and U-joints provided driveline insurance. The 426 Hemi engine was also optional, but at considerably greater expense.

The Super Bee suspension was heavy-duty all the way around. Front torsion bars measured 0.90 inch in diameter. The number of rear leaf springs was increased to six. To limit sway in the corners, there was a 0.94-inch-diameter front stabilizer bar. The shock absorbers and drum brakes were heavy-duty as well. Power front disc brakes were optional. The Super Bee rode on Goodyear Red Streak wide-tread F70x14 tires mounted to wide-rim wheels.

Other equipment not directly tied to performance included a hood with power bulge, but this was nonfunctional. The Super Bee's bumblebee stripes announced this was no ordinary Coronet.

The Super Bee went on sale in February 1968. Prior to introduction, Dodge sent descriptive brochures on the car to all its dealers. The copy was typical of its day, yet it is almost alien to today's car buyer:

"It's the super car for the guy who doesn't want to shy away from GTO's . . . only their high prices.

"Super Bee's for the guy who wants a low-priced performance car that he can drive daily . . . but still take to the track on weekends. One that commands respect when the Christmas tree lights up.

"The Super Bee's the car he's been looking for. It's a gutsy road car with all the goodies to make it a true performance car. If your customer doesn't believe it, tell him you'll meet him with a Super Bee at the local drag strip."

To let performance buffs know the Super Bee was coming, Dodge saturated the performance magazines with full-color, full-page ads. The

A power bulge with simulated hood air intakes was standard in, and exclusive to, the 1968 Coronet R/T and Super Bee.

The Coronet 500 and R/T shared the same interior in 1968. Coronet R/T identification appeared on the interior door panels.

magazines included: *Hot Rod, Car and Driver, Super Stock & Drag Illustrated, Motor Trend, Popular Hot Rodding, Road & Track, Car Life, Drag Strip, Auto Racing, Car Craft* and *Cars*. In addition, Dodge placed black-and-white ads in almost 250 college newspapers.

The Super Bee's performance was comparable to that of the Road Runner. According to Dodge tests, the Super Bee accelerated to 60 mph in 6.8 seconds, and covered the quarter mile in fifteen seconds. The optional Hemi propelled the Super Bee to 60 mph in 6.6 seconds and cut the quarter-mile time by nearly a second. Much of the Hemi's awesome power was wasted literally spinning its wheels leaving the staging lane. These times were confirmed by published road tests.

If you wanted a high-performance Coronet that wasn't quite so spartan, and was a bit faster than the stock Super Bee, there was also the Coronet R/T for 1968. The R/T was again available as either a hardtop or convertible. The R/T was the only Coronet besides the Super Bee to get the power bulge performance hood. R/T medallions were mounted on the front grille, front fenders near the doors and the right rear taillight assembly. You had a choice of bumblebee stripes or body side stripes to ornament your R/T. Nowhere on the exterior of the car was displacement announced. This was counter to the trend at GM and Ford of giving engine displacement on the hood or fenders. Finally, you could order your R/T in one of fifteen exterior colors. An optional vinyl roof was available in black, antique white or antique green.

The R/T interior for 1968 featured new seat designs. The front bucket seats could be ordered with optional color-keyed head restraints, which you could also order for the rear seat. The optional center console was available only in the Coronet 500 and R/T. The console had a map compartment and "bull's eye" courtesy lights near the floor. The standard dash with 150-mph speedometer could be replaced by an optional Rallye Instrument Cluster with clock/tachometer. Virtually all appearance and comfort options were carried over from the previous year.

Horsepower ratings for the 375-hp 440 Magnum and 425-hp Stage II 426 Hemi remained unchanged from 1967. The high-performance dual-

The 1968 Coronet R/T, available as a hardtop or convertible, came standard with the 375-hp 440 Magnum V-8 and a choice of either TorqueFlight automatic or four-speed manual transmission. The Hemi was optional.

exhaust system with 2½-inch exhaust pipes and tuned mufflers with 2¼-inch tail pipes and chromed exhaust tips were the same for both engines.

If you wanted air conditioning in your R/T, it was available only on the 440 Magnum with TorqueFlight automatic transmission. It was not available with the four-speed manual transmission or Hemi-equipped cars.

The heavy-duty Hemi suspension used on the R/T was virtually identical to that used on the Super Bee, except for larger 0.94-inch-diameter front torsion bars, and the extra half-leaf used in the right rear spring to control torque steer.

The Coronet R/T of 1968 was so fully equipped, the only modifications needed to race on the drag strip in stock class were a switch to slicks and running open headers.

Despite its new sheetmetal, Dodge sold only a few hundred more Coronet R/T's in 1968 than it did in 1967. The number of 1968 Coronet R/T's to hit the streets was 10,465.

In terms of performance-generating excitement, 1969 was an even better year for the Scat Pack Coronets. The Super Bee coupe was joined by a hardtop model in 1969, but a Super Bee convertible was still not available. The only visible difference between the 1969 and 1968 models was a switch to a single, broad bumblebee stripe and the addition of a Scat Pack bumblebee medallion in the front grille and on the trunk lid. A small decal giving engine displacement appeared on the side of the front fenders. Performance specifications remained unchanged for the Super Bee in 1969. Base price for the hardtop was $3,697.

Likewise, the Coronet R/T was little changed in appearance or performance. The R/T medallion on the front fenders was eliminated and, in somewhat larger form, appeared as part of the bumblebee stripe. The brochure for the 1969 Coronets showed color renderings of the R/T with

Changes to the 1969 Coronet R/T consisted of a new grille, rectangular turn indicators on the fenders, R/T bumblebee stripe and rear taillight panel.

two simulated air scoops on the rear quarter panels. These were optional on the Super Bee and R/T Coronets.

Both the Super Bee and R/T could be ordered with the new Ramcharger fresh-air induction system. It was identical in function to the Air Grabber fresh-air induction system offered on the Plymouth Road Runner

This 1969 Coronet R/T is equipped with the optional Ramcharger fresh-air induction system with two functional hood scoops.

This rear view was usually all most street racers saw of the 1969 Coronet R/T.

and GTX. The Ramcharger system differed by having two large functional hood scoops that fed the fiberglass plenum bolted to the underside of the hood, which surrounded the oval air cleaner when the hood was closed. You could get cool outside air or warm underhood air by the switch of a lever beneath the dash. Most owners of Super Bees or R/T's with the Ramcharger option left the scoops open. The Ramcharger was standard on Hemi-equipped Coronets.

Another option that had a more direct effect on performance was a wider selection of rear axle ratios for 1969. Dodge essentially had the same rear axle options as Plymouth that year. Depending on the standard or optional engine and transmission, you could improve on the standard rear axle ratio of 3.23:1 by ordering a 3.54:1, 3.55:1, 3.91:1 or 4.10:1 Performance Axle Package. Other heavy-duty equipment, such as radiators, fan shrouds, even whole suspensions, were sometimes part of the package. There was something for every taste and need.

The real excitement for 1969 was the addition of a new model to the Scat Pack. That car was the Coronet Super Bee Six-Pack. In both name and concept, it was one of the wildest muscle cars of the sixties. The heart of the car was its 440 Magnum V-8 with three two-barrel Holley carburetors atop an Edelbrock aluminum intake manifold. This engine churned out 390 hp and 490 pounds-feet of torque.

Engine performance was aided by a fiberglass performance hood with one of the largest scoops to ever go on a performance car. It was also one of the most effective. Of the Six-Pack hood scoop, Chrysler's Dick Maxwell said, "It wasn't stylish, but it worked." The hood, in fact, was shared by the Plymouth Road Runner 440 6-bbl; it was painted flat-black and held in place by four chrome hood pins, which allowed the entire hood to be quickly removed. In most instances, the hood was simply placed temporarily on the roof.

The Super Bee Six-Pack came with a choice of either four-speed manual or TorqueFlight automatic transmission. The rear end was the ultimate setup. The 9¾-inch Dana 60 rear axle had a ratio of 4.10:1 and came with Sure-Grip. The Goodyear G70x15 Polyglas tires were mounted on six-inch-wide steel wheels, painted black and bolted by chrome lug nuts.

The Super Bee Six-Pack practically screamed *drag strip*. Its appearance and equipment specifications made it clear this car really had only one purpose in life—to race toward the quarter-mile timing lights. It was one of the best street/strip machines ever to roll off an assembly line, from a company known for its street/strip machines.

The Ramcharger fresh-air package was optional on the Coronet Super Bee and R/T, but came standard when the 426 Hemi was ordered in either car.

The Six-Pack name deserves particular mention. The name, inspired by the six-barrel induction system, was the brainchild of Bob Osborn at BBD&O (Batten, Barten, Durstine & Osborn). Dodge's advertising agency cleverly used the car's name in an ad with a wide-angle color photo of the Super Bee Six-Pack which opened with the words, "Six Pack to go!" To a young man in his late teens or early twenties, this ad was enough to incite mechanical lust.

Also, the name seemed to catch the attention of the enthusiast magazines more than the Plymouth Road Runner 440 6-bbl. *Car and Driver* was among the first to drive the car, but the magazine didn't actually perform a road test. In the tongue-in-cheek style of writing for which *Car and Driver* is famous (or infamous), writer Joe Whitlock had some good ol' boys in the deep south drive the car to see if it would make a good "liquor car" to run moonshine. Wrote Whitlock, "After a day of bootleg turns, dirt roads, trips up creek beds, the consensus was that 'It'll run like hell.'" The article was appropriately titled "A Six-Pack Full of 'Shine.'"

On a more serious note, *Motorcade* magazine did a legitimate test of the car in its July 1969 issue. Weighing 3,790 pounds and equipped with the TorqueFlight automatic transmission, the Super Bee Six-Pack did 0-60 mph in 6.6 seconds and covered the quarter mile in 13.65 seconds at 105.14 mph at the Orange County International Raceway.

It's interesting to note that the Super Bee Six-Pack driven by *Car and Driver* did not have the simulated air scoops on the rear quarter panels, while *Motorcade*'s test car did have the scoops.

There weren't many new options added to the already extensive list. The new fifteen-inch cast aluminum road wheel was one of them. However, not many Super Bees or R/T's were ordered with this wheel; most buyers opted for the chromed steel fourteen-inch road wheel.

The Coronet R/T and Super Bee finished out the sixties as two of Dodge's most formidable and affordable muscle cars. Sales for the Coronet R/T in 1969 dropped more than 3,000 units to 7,238. Those sales were probably lost to the more attractive Charger R/T, which recorded an increase in sales in 1969 of almost an identical number of units. Nearly 28,000 Super Bees were sold in 1969. In fact, 1969 was to be the best year for combined sales of the Dodge Scat Pack.

For 1970, the Coronet received all-new front end sheetmetal. It is hard to believe that a styling studio that produced such handsome cars as the 1970 Charger and Challenger could also produce a car as unattractive as the 1970 Coronet. More subtle restyling was done to the shallow scoop on the rear quarter panels.

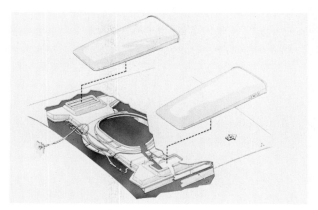

The 1969 Ramcharger fresh-air induction system was similar to Plymouth's Air Grabber, but the Ramcharger had more effective hood scoops.

Both the Coronet Super Bee and the Coronet R/T returned for 1970. The Super Bee was offered as a two-door coupe for $3,012 or a two-door hardtop for $3,074. Both Super Bees were $64 less than the year before. This was achieved by substituting a fully synchronized three-speed manual transmission with floor shifter and making the four-speed manual transmission optional. A few options from 1969 were made standard on the 1970 Super Bee. These included fiberglass-belted wide-tread tires, lane change signal, key-left-in-ignition buzzer and three-way ignition, steering and transmission lock. The last three items were standard in all Coronets.

Super Bees that year were quickly identified by the new power bulge hood with two razor-edge, nonfunctional scoops. Super Bee appeared on the sides of the power bulge. Other identification was a choice of either the traditional bumblebee stripe or a longitudinal tape stripe in the shape of a C on the rear quarter panels. Only the longitudinal tape stripe featured the bumblebee figure. The bumblebee figure appeared again on the trim panel between the taillights.

The standard powerplant was again the 335-hp four-barrel 383. The optional engines included the 440 Six-Pack or the 426 Hemi. The 440 Six-Pack Super Bee did not come with a fiberglass hood and scoop in 1970. Dodge reverted to a steel hood that was standard on the Super Bee. However, the Ramcharger fresh-air induction system was optional. When you ordered the 426 Hemi, the Ramcharger was standard.

The 1970 Coronet R/T hardtop featured rear quarter panel scoops, different taillights and R/T medallions to distinguish it from the Super Bee.

The Super Bee suspension that year was unchanged. It was equipped with Rallye Suspension, a special handling package that included heavy-duty torsion bars, front stabilizer bar and heavy-duty rear springs.

The 1970 Coronet R/T was again offered as a hardtop for $3,569 and a convertible for $3,785. The exterior was identical to the Super Bee except for the R/T medallions on the front of the hood, the bogus scoops bolted to the rear quarter panels with R/T medallions and an R/T medallion on the taillight trim panel. The Coronet R/T also had different taillights. The

The 1970 Coronet Super Bee could be ordered with an optional rear deck spoiler, Tuff steering wheel and new hood-mounted 8000 rpm tachometer.

This 1970 Coronet Super Bee coupe is shown with the optional wire wheel covers, alternate tape stripe treatment and functional Ramcharger hood scoops with 440 Magnum V-8 power.

standard and only bumblebee stripe was the same as that on the Super Bee. The longitudinal tape stripe was not offered on the R/T. Displacement was not given anywhere on the R/T's exterior. It wasn't necessary; by 1970 R/T was synonymous with 440 cubic inches. The TorqueFlight automatic transmission was standard, with the four-speed manual transmission an extra-cost option.

Both the 440 Six-Pack and the 426 Hemi were optional in the Coronet R/T. The Coronet's extra-heavy-duty suspension was also unchanged from 1969.

You could order your Super Bee or R/T in one of thirteen standard colors but these cars looked most effective in one of the five optional extra-cost performance colors, which included Plum Crazy, Sublime, Go-Mango, Hemi Orange and Banana. These could be contrasted by an optional vinyl roof in black, white, green or Gator Grain.

One reason performance cars such as the Super Bee and the R/T were so affordable was that they did not come with the comfort and convenience accessories that are standard on many of today's cars. Power steering, power brakes, tinted glass, front disc brakes and four-speed manual transmission were optional. This kept the cars affordable to the young buyers and allowed them to go as far as their budgets would allow.

In a brochure covering the 1970 Scat Pack offerings titled *Big News From Scat City*, Dodge also offered five Scat Packages to be installed after the sale or on older Mopars. The Showboat was a dress-up kit that included chromed valve covers, oil filler cap, air cleaner, hood pins and locks, and

The 1970 Dodge Coronet Six-Pack 440-ci V-8 had power almost equivalent to the much more expensive 426 Hemi.

chromed road wheels. The Read-Out included a full-sweep tachometer, oil pressure gauge and fuel pressure gauge. The Kruncher included a higher numerical ring gear and pinion, matching speedometer pinion and Hurst shifter. The Bee-Liever included a high-rise manifold and carburetor, street camshaft and steel tubing headers. Finally, the Top Eliminator included a 1969-style Six-Pack fiberglass hood with scoop and hood pins, Six-Pack manifold and carburetors, transistorized ignition, electric fuel pump and cool can—a coiled fuel line that could be packed with ice around it and resulted in fractionally improved times at the strip.

While 1970 was a high-water mark in Dodge performance car offerings, the insurance industry began its crackdown on such cars, making them very costly to insure. Consequently, sales for the 1970 Coronet Super Bee dropped to 15,506, while sales of the Coronet R/T came to only 2,615.

In 1971, Dodge consolidated the Coronet and Charger lines. The Coronet was now available only in a four-door sedan and station wagon. Thus, there was no Coronet Super Bee or Coronet R/T in 1971. Instead, Dodge added a Super Bee model to the Charger line, to complement the Charger R/T that year.

Of the two high-performance 1970 Coronet models, only the R/T was offered as a convertible. These are extremely rare.

CHAPTER EIGHT

Barracuda 1970-1974

*P*lymouth stylists had been hard at work coming up with the third-generation Barracuda for 1970. The car was completely redesigned both inside and out. Wheelbase remained the same but overall width was increased more than five inches and front and rear tracks were increased three inches, primarily to accept the massive 426 Hemi and 60-series tires to handle all that extra weight and power.

Although some elements of the previous design were vaguely apparent, the new Barracuda was much more clean, crisp and taut. The long hood/short deck theme was more obvious and the high trunk, short roof and smooth, undisturbed sheetmetal gave it a more-balanced look. Plymouth stylists paid particular attention to design and manufacturing details to maintain the uncluttered theme of the car. The windshield wipers were now recessed. The front end sheetmetal was carried right to the leading edge, then sharply turned under. The same was done to the rear of the car. Door handles were flush. The rectangular dual exhaust tips exited through the rear end sheetmetal on the 'Cuda model.

There were three distinct models for 1970: Barracuda, Gran Coupe and 'Cuda. Each model was available as either a two-door hardtop or convertible. There was not a fastback body style as before.

You could order the new Plymouth ponycar in one of eighteen exterior colors. Five were extra-cost colors: TorRed, In Violet (metallic), Lemon Twist, Lime Light and Vitamin C. Optional vinyl roofs came in black, white, green, Gator Grain and two floral-pattern Mod Tops carried over from the previous year.

It was the 'Cuda that was of interest to Mopar enthusiasts. Previously, the Barracuda had picked up the slang name 'Cuda among Woodward Avenue cruisers as well as others around the country, so Plymouth adopted 'Cuda as a tough-sounding name for a new model appropriate to its image. With the 'Cuda, Plymouth addressed a specific market it hadn't before: street racers who wanted a high-performance Plymouth in the Ford Mustang Cobra-Jet league.

The 'Cuda was one of five cars that comprised the Rapid Transit System. In the October 1969 issue of *Car and Driver,* as well as other magazines, Plymouth ran an ad that read: "The Rapid Transit System Announced." The other cars in the RTS, as enthusiasts called it for short, were the GTX, Sport Fury GT, Road Runner and Valiant Duster 340. As later ads would point out, the Rapid Transit System was more than a collection of cars; it was factory-sponsored racing in practically all its forms

—SuperCar Clinics hosted by the likes of Sox & Martin and Don Grotheer for the benefit of high-performance Plymouth owners, availability of performance parts through your Plymouth dealer and tips on how to make your car go faster. You could say it was "service after the sale," with the enthusiast in mind.

The 'Cuda came standard with a high-performance four-barrel 383 rated at 335 hp at 5200 rpm. Optional engines included the 275-hp four-barrel 340, the 375-hp four-barrel 440, the 390-hp six-barrel 440 and the 425-hp eight-barrel Hemi.

The distinguishing feature of the 'Cuda was the standard performance hood, which sported two beautiful, rakish, nonfunctional scoops. Because the hood was stamped steel, plastic moldings had to be used at the "openings" to resolve the undercut problem. Hood pins were standard on the 'Cuda, as were two high-intensity driving lights mounted below the front bumper. The performance hood and hood pins were optional on the Barracuda and Gran Coupe.

Identification on the Barracuda and Gran Coupe came in the form of chrome script on the front fenders. On the 'Cuda, the sole identification was the word 'Cuda in silver on the right of the rear license plate holder. Also, the recessed rear end was painted flat-black on 'Cudas.

An interesting appearance option was the elastomeric front and rear bumpers. (This consisted of taking an unchromed bumper, molding a smooth skin of urethane over it, and painting it.) Two packages were available. One was the front bumper in any one of nine body colors with racing mirrors. The other package had the front and rear bumpers and racing mirrors in Rallye Red only.

Another appearance option announced engine displacement. An inverted "hockey stick" flat-black paint stripe started above the door han-

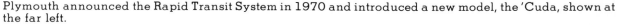

Plymouth announced the Rapid Transit System in 1970 and introduced a new model, the 'Cuda, shown at the far left.

dle, followed the fenderline toward the rear of the car and, just after turning down, read 340, 383, 440 or Hemi.

The other way to announce engine displacement was with the functional shaker scoop, available as an option only on the 'Cuda in the Plymouth line. This was a corporate scoop, optional also on the Dodge Chal-

The interior of the 1970 Barracuda was clean and functional. A 150 mph speedometer was standard. The center console with TorqueFlight automatic transmission (shown) or four-speed manual transmission was optional.

The 1970 Hemi 'Cuda came standard with the functional shaker hood scoop. The 'Cuda was available as a two-door hardtop or convertible.

lenger. It was available with all high-performance engines in the 'Cuda. Engine displacement was also given on the scoops of the standard performance hood.

Plymouth was quick to supplement the option list for the 'Cuda. A rear spoiler, code J81, could be ordered for $34.80. Like the shaker scoop, this was a corporate option also available on certain other Plymouth and Dodge performance cars. A backlight louver option, code A67, was available for $175.05. It included black louvers, black vinyl roof, black backlight molding and right and left color-keyed racing mirrors. If you wanted to jazz up your plain Barracuda or Gran Coupe with a 'Cuda performance hood, code J54, it cost you only $20.95. The hood pins, code J45, cost $15.40.

Plymouth fans did not have to pay extra for heavy-duty suspensions on their 'Cudas; they came standard. Said Larry Shepard of Chrysler, "We offered our cars with a complete package, not just a big motor. The guy at the local drive-in could talk about his Mopar with Super Stock springs, heavy-duty rear axle, TorqueFlight transmission with high-stall converter and so on, and the Chevy guys didn't have any of that. All they could do was point to SS on the side of the car and talk about the motor."

'Cudas powered by the 340 or 383 came with heavy-duty 0.90-inch-diameter front torsion bars with a spring rate of 113 pounds per inch, heavy-duty rear leaf springs with a spring rate of 129 pounds per inch, heavy-duty 0.94-inch-diameter front stabilizer bar, 0.75-inch-diameter rear stabi- the 440 engines or the 426 Hemi came with extra-heavy-duty 0.92-inch-diameter front torsion bars with a spring rate of 124 pounds per inch, extra-heavy-duty rear leaf springs with five full leaves plus two half-leaves on the left side and six full leaves on the right side with a spring rate of 148 pounds per inch, heavy-duty 0.94-inch-diameter front stabilizer bar, no rear stabilizer bar and extra-heavy-duty shock absorbers.

The 1970 Hemi 'Cuda was called the Rapid Transit Authority in Plymouth advertising. This one was appropriately photographed at Orange County International Raceway.

Transmissions and differentials were also up to the task. A heavy-duty three-speed manual transmission and heavy-duty rear axle with Chrysler-built 8¾-inch-diameter ring gear came standard with 340- and 383-powered 'Cudas. The high-upshift TorqueFlight automatic transmission came standard in 'Cudas with 440 or 426 Hemi engines, and power reached the pavement through an extra-heavy-duty Dana 60 rear axle with 9¾-inch-diameter ring gear. On 'Cudas with 340 or 383 engines and three-speed or optional four-speed manual transmissions, a 3.23:1 axle ratio was standard. You could order 3.55:1 or 3.91:1 axle ratios with four-speed manual transmissions as part of the Performance Axle Packages. If you went up in engine displacement, a 3.54:1 axle ratio was standard on four-speed stick 'Cudas, with an optional 4.10:1 rear axle ratio. If you ordered the TorqueFlight automatic transmission, a 3.23:1 axle ratio was standard, with a choice of optional 3.55:1 or 4.10:1 ratios as part of the Performance Axle Packages which included Sure-Grip differentials.

The louvered backlight, a worthwhile option on the 'Cuda, reduced glare and moisture. It was hinged to permit window cleaning.

This optional steel road wheel was available on many Plymouth and Dodge performance cars.

The optional rear spoiler offered more performance image than function.

The four-speed manual transmission came with a Hurst shifter and pistol grip that fit the hand perfectly.

'Cudas were equipped with larger drum brakes than those on the Barracuda. The Barracuda came with 10x2½-inch front and rear drums having 195.2 square inches swept area. 'Cudas came with 11x3-inch front and 11x2½-inch rear drums with 234.1 square inches swept area. Front disc brakes were optional.

To complete the package, the 'Cudas with 383 or 440 engines came standard with F70x14-inch white-letter tires on six-inch rims. E60x15-

The production AAR 'Cuda of 1970 was the wildest-looking and best-handling 'Cuda built. Offered only for one year, good examples command high prices.

The 1970 'Cuda's good looks extended to the flush door handles and sculpted interior door panels.

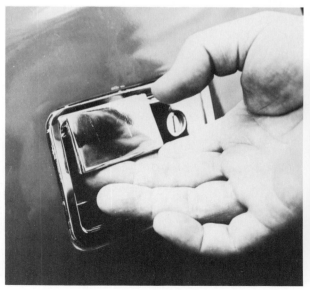 

inch tires on seven-inch rims were optional but came standard on the 340 four-barrel 'Cuda. The Hemi 'Cuda came equipped with F60x15-inch tires on seven-inch rims.

Nestled among all this heavy-duty hardware was a high-performance dual exhaust system which, on the 'Cuda with standard 383 V-8, featured 2¼-inch exhaust pipes with tuned low restriction mufflers and 2¼-inch tail pipes. The 340 'Cuda got the same system. 'Cudas powered by the 440 or Hemi engines received 2½-inch exhaust pipes, tuned low-restriction mufflers and 2¼-inch tail pipes.

The 1970 Hemi 'Cuda was the rarest and most powerful Barracuda to prowl the streets. The functional hood scoop was standard on the Hemi 'Cuda.

Base list price for the standard 'Cuda hardtop was $3,164. The list price for the 'Cuda convertible was $3,433. Sales of the 1970 Barracuda ran fifty-three percent over 1969.

The 'Cuda was a popular test car in 1970. *Road Test* magazine put a 383-powered 'Cuda through its paces. With a TorqueFlight automatic transmission and a Sure-Grip 3.91:1 rear end, the car did the quarter mile in 14.40 seconds at 98.87 mph. *Car Craft* tested a Hemi 'Cuda with four-speed manual transmission and a 3.54:1 Sure-Grip rear axle. This car did the quarter mile in 13.10 seconds at over 107 mph. *Motor Trend* got behind the wheel of a 440 6-bbl 'Cuda with the same axle setup as the *Car Craft* test car, and did the quarter mile in 14.44 seconds at 99.88 mph, but others recorded better times.

Many magazines suspected that their test cars received factory super tuning to the ignition and/or carburetor to enhance test results. Chrysler was no exception. Such tuning on Mopars was usually limited to replacing the distributor springs and weights and bumping the spark advance. These modifications greatly improved drivability and performance. In truth, any enthusiast could perform these same modifications and achieve similar results.

There was yet another way to go in a 'Cuda for 1970. In February of that year, Plymouth announced the availability of the AAR 'Cuda by late March. The SCCA-sanctioned Trans-Am racing series drew a great deal of attention in 1969, and Plymouth wanted a piece of the action. Said Chrysler's Larry Shepard, "We felt we had better cars and wanted to show it. You have to compete, even if you don't win, to get attention." Mark Donohue had raced Camaros and switched to AMC Javelins. Parnelli Jones drove a Mustang, and Jerry Titus drove a Firebird. Both Chrysler divisions wanted

Don "The Snake" Prudhomme campaigned a Hemi-powered Barracuda funny car in 1970. He also raced a Hemi-powered fuel dragster that year.

to gain high visibility with their respective ponycars, and the Trans-Am series was one of the best ways to do it.

To enter the series, Plymouth had to build 2,500 street versions of its racing 'Cuda. Plymouth contracted Dan Gurney and his company, All American Racers, to build and race the Trans-Am 'Cuda. Plymouth then contracted Creative Industries to design and manufacture the fiberglass hood and rear spoiler that were to go on both the racing and street versions. The AAR 'Cuda was conceived to resemble the racing car as closely as practicality, legality and cost would allow.

The sales code for the AAR 'Cuda was A53. The engine was unique to the car: a 340-ci block with reinforced main webs and filled pan rails, six-barrel carburetion using three two-barrel Holley carburetors on an Edelbrock aluminum intake manifold, special cylinder heads and valve train. Dodge used this same engine in its 1970 Challenger T/A, but the 340 six-barrel V-8 was not available in any other Dodge or Plymouth. The choice of either the TorqueFlight or four-speed manual transmission was standard. The car was equipped with a 3.55:1 rear axle ratio with Sure-Grip; a 3.91:1 ratio was optional. Front disc brakes were standard. The AAR 'Cuda suspension included special front and rear stabilizer bars and heavy-duty shock absorbers. Special heavy-duty rear springs raised the rear end to make room for a Trans-Am-type exhaust system with side outlets, and provided room for extra-large rear G60x15 tires. Front tires were E60x15. Plymouth's sharp Road Wheels were standard.

The AAR 'Cuda's appearance on the street made heads turn. The grille, hood, cowl and fender tops were flat-black. Ornamentation included a black strobe stripe which ran the length of the car on both sides, ending at the rear in an AAR 'Cuda decal with the AAR in the form of the Dan Gurney All-American Racers crest in red, white and blue.

These road rockets were a blast to drive on the street. The AAR 'Cuda was much better balanced than the big-block 'Cuda's and, with its quick-ratio manual steering, was an exciting machine on twisty roads. The engine, conservatively rated at 290 hp, was more than adequate to propel the car.

The full-race AAR 'Cuda got off to a slow start in the 1970 Trans-Am series and driver Swede Savage did not place well. Plymouth did not return to the series the following year.

Of course, most owners really thrashed these cars, and few of the 2,800 AAR 'Cudas built that remain are in good condition. Those that are, are worth considerably more than the original selling price.

Plymouth had some of the wildest advertisements of the super car era. The advertising agency responsible for producing these memorable ads was Young & Rubicam. Jim Ramsey and Joe Schulte were the account executives. One of the best ads for the 'Cuda featured a color illustration by Bob Grossman, known for his unique airbrush style. A Hemi 'Cuda spread over two pages was wildly distorted, in typical Grossman fashion, shown with Hemi Orange paint and black vinyl roof. Headlights and driving lights were blazing. And almost erupting through the hood was a shaker

The shaker hood scoop was available in 1970 and 1971 'Cudas with 340, 383, 440 and 426 Hemi engines.

The 'Cuda ragtop was last offered in 1971. This one is shown with the standard performance hood. Note the optional color-keyed elastomeric bumpers.

scoop of mammoth proportions, glowing ominously from within, with a curious purple vapor being drawn into the "nostrils" of the scoop—sniffing out the poor, unfortunate competition, perhaps? The tag line above this outrageous, eye-catching illustration read, "The Rapid Transit Authority." The first paragraph of ad copy read, "It's Hemi 'Cuda. Our angriest, slipperiest-looking body shell, wrapped around ol' King Kong hisself." This indeed was the golden age of supercar advertising!

The 'Cuda was a hit with professional and amateur drag racers. It had a two-inch-shorter wheelbase than the 110-inch-wheelbase Challenger. While the 440 Magnum and Hemi-powered 'Cudas were not nimble-handling cars, they were ferocious in a straight line. The drag racing duo of Sox & Martin campaigned a 1970 Hemi 'Cuda in the Super Stock class. With the help of co-driver Herb McCandless, the team won seventeen major events around the country. Sox & Martin was the most active race team of the Hemi 'Cuda in 1970.

Because the AAR 'Cuda was practically a mid-1970 introduction, it did not fare well on the Trans-Am circuit. Driver Swede Savage had his hands full behind the wheel of the AAR 'Cuda, for he had to compete against the likes of Mark Donohue driving the Roger Penske-prepared Javelin, Parnelli Jones in a Boss 302, and Jim Hall piloting a Camaro Z-28 (all with more development time behind them). By the end of the 1970 Trans-Am season, the Plymouth-backed Dan Gurney team finished in the back of the pack.

Total Barracuda sales for 1970 came to 30,267.

All models and body styles were carried over for 1971, except the AAR 'Cuda. The primary changes to the Barracuda were aesthetic. The car now had four headlights instead of two, and the road lights were optional. The grille resembled a cheese grater, with six large cutouts in a silver-tone finish. The rear end panel and taillight assembly were new. In addition, the '71 'Cuda had four small simulated louvers on the front fenders. If you ordered the elastomeric bumper group, the front grille was color-keyed to the bumper and body.

The 1971 Rapid Transit System brochure featured a 'Cuda 340, with Air Grabber shaker hood and rear spoiler as a rendering, not a photograph. Barely visible in the color illustration were two small front spoilers. The brochure showed and mentioned the availability of the rear spoiler, but it made no mention of the front spoilers, which may not have been offered.

Interior seating was all new for 1971. Optionally available on the 'Cuda was an all-vinyl split bench seat with center armrest available in blue, green, white, black or tan. Two other seating options were offered: genuine

The Rapid Transit System Caravan toured the country, appearing at custom car shows, in 1971. This customized 'Cuda 440 was one of the creations on display.

leather bucket seats in black or tan, or cloth-and-vinyl bucket seats which gave better grip during cornering and were cooler in summer.

Engine offerings continued virtually unchanged. The standard 383 four-barrel V-8 in the 'Cuda suffered a one-point drop in compression ratio to 8.5:1, to run on regular gas. Its gross horsepower was down from 335 to 300, but this was also taken at 4800 rpm, 400 rpm lower than the previous year. Net horsepower, a more realistic rating of rear wheel horsepower then being adopted by the automotive industry, was 250. The high-performance four-barrel 340 specifications were identical except for a 0.2-point drop in compression; horsepower was unaltered. The 440 four-barrel V-8 was dropped from the 'Cuda line. The 440 six-barrel V-8 was still offered, but it too dropped slightly in compression, from 10.5:1 to 10.3:1, with a subsequent drop of five horsepower. The specifications for the 426 Hemi were unchanged. Interestingly, the unsilenced air cleaners on the 440 six-barrel and 426 Hemi engines were not available in California because of that state's new drive-by noise regulations. A quieter air cleaner was used to muffle induction roar on those engines bound for California.

Base price for the 1971 'Cuda hardtop was $3,155. The 'Cuda convertible listed for $3,412. This was the last year of the 'Cuda convertible.

Plymouth offered huge rear quarter panel graphics announcing engine displacement in 1971.

Sales figures for the Barracuda dropped dramatically in 1971. Only 17,013 cars were sold. These figures spelled doom to the Rapid Transit System and other makes in general and the high-performance engines of the 'Cuda in particular.

In 1972, Mopar enthusiasts were in for a shock. The 426 Hemi, six-barrel 440 and even the 383 engines were dropped from the 'Cuda line. The standard engine was now a two-barrel 318 V-8 with single exhaust. The transmission was the three-speed manual with floor-mounted shifter. The 240-hp four-barrel 340 V-8 with dual exhaust was optional and the only way to go if you wanted respectable acceleration. The four-speed manual transmission was available, as were the pistol-grip Hurst shifter and the Sure-Grip differential. When the big-block engines were dropped from the 'Cuda after 1971, the strong Dana 60 rear axle and choice of axle ratios were also dropped because they were no longer needed.

The interior of the 1971 Barracuda was less flamboyant than the 1970 'Cuda. Note the collapsible steering column.

This 1972 'Cuda is shown with the optional blacked-out hood treatment. A four-barrel 340 V-8 was the largest engine available that year in the Barracuda.

Stylistically, the '72 'Cuda reverted back to two headlights and a grille almost identical to the '70 model, except for slots in the center grille divider. Round taillights made their appearance. The 'Cuda logo shifted from the right of the license plate recess to the left. Sixteen exterior colors were available and three interior colors were offered. A blacked-out hood treatment was optional on the 'Cuda; the hood and fender tops were flat-black but the area leading up to and including the hood scoops remained the body color. Black body side stripes were standard. The front fender louvers of the previous year disappeared. The driving lights mounted below the bumper returned, however. The list price for the 'Cuda hardtop dropped to $3,029.

The standard bucket seats in the 1972 Barracuda offered better grip than the seats in 1971.

Changes to the 1973 Barracuda were limited to appearance, such as the body side tape stripe shown. The front grille was also new.

Despite the bottom falling out of the performance market, an ad for the Rapid Transit System did appear in 1972. There were only three cars in the System now: the Road Runner, the Duster 340 and the 'Cuda. The two-page ad compared the cars of the Rapid Transit System to the plain vanilla versions from which they were derived—the Satellite, Duster and Barracuda—and noted how similar they were under the skin. Curiously, sales picked up that year—19,090 Plymouth E-bodies were sold in 1972.

The story was pretty much the same for 1973. The 'Cuda's image was downgraded from performance to merely sporty. This was exemplified by the brochure describing the Duster/Valiant and Barracuda. A red 'Cuda with black vinyl roof and side stripe and a gold Barracuda were shown parked near a baseball diamond in the 1973 brochure. Standing behind the 'Cuda was a young couple with a baby in the wife's arms, and an elderly woman—perhaps a grandmother—was holding a baby bottle to feed the little tyke. The message was clear: The youth that had been enflamed by the Rapid Transit Authority was now a family man and wanted something more practical.

Except for reinforced bumpers in the form of rubber-tipped over-riders to comply with government regulations, the '73 'Cuda's appearance was unchanged. The same number of exterior colors was available.

Improvements were made to the interior seating. The brochure stated: "The new standard Barracuda and 'Cuda all-vinyl bucket seat is of an entirely new construction, and comfort is engineered in with computerized analysis. Spring deflection, stress levels, and fatigue characteristics are carefully correlated for ideal support and comfort." Apparently, all this

A shot of a rare 1974 'Cuda. Fewer than 4,000 Plymouth E-bodies were built before production was stopped.

was a concern to new 'Cuda buyers. Certainly, little mention was made of the performance aspect of the 'Cuda. Interior colors were blue, green, black and white. All performance-related options were carried over from 1972.

Sales rose again for the Barracuda; 21,338 units were sold in 1973. The 'Cuda two-door hardtop sold for $3,120.

Plymouth surprised 'Cuda fans by introducing a larger optional engine for 1974. The 340 V-8 was dropped and a 360 V-8 took its place having a healthy 245 hp with 320 pounds-feet of torque—a substantial increase over the output of the 340 V-8 of 1973. Few prospective 'Cuda buyers got to sample this engine with the usual retinue of performance options, however. Plymouth stopped its E-body production in 1974. Less than 4,000 Barracudas of all types were sold. Chrysler/Plymouth couldn't justify the time and expense of outfitting its low-selling E-body with 5 mph bumpers, catalytic converters and other banes to a performance car's existence. Thus, the 1974 'Cuda was the last and rarest of a fine line of performance cars.

Nevertheless, these cars remain popular vehicles in sanctioned drag racing and have proved to be every bit as fearsome and tenacious as their namesake.

CHAPTER NINE

Challenger 1970-1974

*I*n the fall of 1966, Chrysler management decided to meet the market need for a car to compete with the newly introduced Mercury Cougar, a personal luxury sporty car. Dodge was given the job and the program was headed by Harry Cheeseborough, senior vice president of Styling and Product Planning. The task of coming up with the all-important body design belonged to Bill Brownlie, then chief of design in the Dodge studio.

By the early part of 1967, a full-size finished clay model was produced to allow the young stylists a chance to gain a basic concept of the new car's length, height, wheelbase and interior size. It reflected the long hood, short rear deck design in vogue. Brownlie turned his stylists loose to come up with drawings incorporating their ideas for the unnamed car. In numerous meetings, ideas were kicked around and the first styling clay model using their ideas took shape. A total of four full-size clay models were made with the right and left sides of each shaped differently to offer eight separate concepts. Things did not go smoothly, however. There were still differing opinions on how the car should look. The time for presenting the design to top management was drawing near.

Brownlie felt he should back up the styling studio and came up with some sketches the weekend prior to the meeting as insurance. He had models made from the sketches, as he conceived the car, ready for the meeting. It was Brownlie's body design that was chosen and it remained virtually unaltered for production. Subsequent detailing to the extreme front and rear ends was handled by the styling studio. His suggestion for the name Challenger was also adopted because of its association with the Charger.

Performance enthusiasm in the market had surged to such an extent in 1968 and 1969, that it was decided to market the 1970 Challenger predominantly as a performance car.

Dodge was the last of the manufacturers to join the ponycar race, so Challenger, introduced in the fall of 1969, was an appropriate name. Unlike its brother, the Barracuda, the Challenger had no ancestry. Nevertheless, when it hit the showrooms, Mopar fans were understandably excited by the newest addition to the Dodge Scat Pack.

Although the Challenger shared all window glass with the 1970 Barracuda, it had a strikingly different look. Its contours were more sculpted, and it featured a prominent S-bend beltline crease. The Challenger had a four-headlight arrangement in contrast to the Barracuda's two headlights. It also differed dimensionally. Both cars had the same front and rear track of 59.7 inches and 60.7 inches respectively, but the Challenger had a 110-inch wheelbase, two inches longer than the Barracuda's.

There were six distinct Challenger models: a two-door hardtop for $2,851, a two-door convertible for $3,120, the SE two-door hardtop for $3,083, the R/T two-door hardtop for $3,266, the R/T SE two-door hardtop for $3,498 and the R/T convertible for $3,535. Adding a convertible to the line gave prospective ponycar buyers a broader selection than did the competition. By 1970, the Pontiac Firebird and Chevrolet Camaro no longer were offered in a convertible. American Motors never had offered the Javelin or AMX in a convertible. The Ford Mustang was available as a convertible, but not in performance trim like the Mach 1. If you wanted a powerful ragtop ponycar, the Challenger R/T convertible and the 'Cuda convertible were the only ways to go.

Dodge leaned heavily on the Challenger's performance image and backed it up with substance. The second page of the 1970 brochure read: "The SixPack. It snarls, it quivers, it leaps vast prairies at a single bound." This sounds outrageous today, but in 1970, the youthful buyers believed it without blinking because it wasn't far from the truth. The 440 Six-Pack Challenger R/T had a snarling exhaust note, the optional shaker hood scoop did quiver, and when you floored this beast, its acceleration was almost frightening.

The 440 Six-Pack engine was only one of nine available in the Challenger that year. Dodge restricted certain engines to specific Challenger models.

The Challenger came standard with a choice of either the 145-hp 225-ci one-barrel slant six or the 230-hp 318-ci two-barrel V-8. A 275-hp

Before it was christened Challenger, the first full-size clay model simply used the word "Name." Conceived to compete with the Mercury Cougar, the Challenger was later marketed as a performance car.

These photos show the dual nature of the Challenger full-size clay models as the car literally took shape in the Dodge styling studio. A Mercury Cougar is parked next to it.

four-barrel 340 V-8, a 290-hp two-barrel V-8 and a 330-hp four-barrel 383 V-8 were optional in the Challenger and Challenger SE. A three-speed synchronized manual transmission with floor shift was standard on all these engines except the two-barrel 383, which came with the TorqueFlight automatic transmission as a mandatory option. The four-speed synchronized manual transmission was optional on some of these engines. Real performance buffs skipped all this and aimed for the Challenger R/T.

The Challenger R/T came standard with the 335-hp four-barrel 383 Magnum V-8, three-on-the-floor synchromesh manual transmission, heavy-duty Rallye suspension, heavy-duty drum brakes, Rallye Instrument Cluster (which included a 150 mph speedometer, oil pressure gauge and 8000 rpm tachometer) and a performance hood with two hood scoops. These hood scoops were open to the engine bay, but did not feed directly to the air cleaner. You could specify a longitudinal or bumblebee tape stripe at no extra cost.

The three optional engines in the Challenger R/T were the 375-hp four-barrel 440 Magnum, the 390-hp 440 Six-Pack with three two-barrel Holley carburetors and the 425-hp 426 Hemi with two four-barrel carburetors. An extra-heavy-duty suspension came standard with these engines, as well as bigger drum brakes.

A range of axle ratios was optional on the Challenger R/T. If you ordered the Trak Pak for $148.15, you got a 3.54:1 ratio. The Super Trak Pak for $235.65 stuffed a 4.10:1 rear end between the tires. Both these packages included the Sure-Grip limited-slip differential. If you ordered the four-speed manual transmission with Hurst shifter behind your 440 or 426 Hemi, the extra-heavy-duty Dana 60 rear axle with 9¾-inch ring gear came standard to withstand the brutal loads it would be subjected to—on the street or the strip. The four-speed transmission came with wood-grain

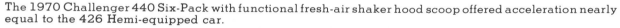

The 1970 Challenger 440 Six-Pack with functional fresh-air shaker hood scoop offered acceleration nearly equal to the 426 Hemi-equipped car.

custom-grip shifter that fit perfectly in your hand and was unbeatable for image. The optional TorqueFlight automatic transmission could soak up the immense torque and power of these engines, so the Dana 60 rear axle wasn't necessary with this transmission.

Dodge also selected the appropriate Goodyear tires to match displacement. The high-performance 340 V-8-equipped Challenger came with E60x15 tires on seven-inch-wide rims. All Challengers fitted with the 383 V-8's, except the R/T, came with F78x14 tires on five-inch-wide wheels. The R/T came shod with F70x14 black sidewall tires with raised white lettering on six-inch-wide wheels; but if you ordered the Hemi, you got F60x15 Goodyear tires with raised white letters on seven-inch-wide wheels.

The Challenger was available in eighteen exterior colors. Five of these were optional High-Impact colors: Plum Crazy, Sub Lime, Go-Mango, Hemi Orange and Top Banana, later joined by Panther Pink and Green-Go. You could order these wild colors on your Challenger and get away with it because they looked so absolutely right on the car. As if these weren't enough, you could specify horizontal florescent body striping, color-keyed to Panther Pink or Green-Go on R/T models at no extra cost.

Few Challengers were seen without a contrasting vinyl roof, in black, white, green or Gator Grain. This came standard on the SE and R/T SE models, which also included an overhead interior consolette with indicator lights reading door ajar, low fuel and seat belt. Also included were leather

The standard instrument panel of the 1970 Challenger was designed to exceed federal safety standards. The Rallye Cluster, standard on the Challenger R/T and optional on other models, added a tachometer, clock and oil pressure gauge, and had a wood-grain finish.

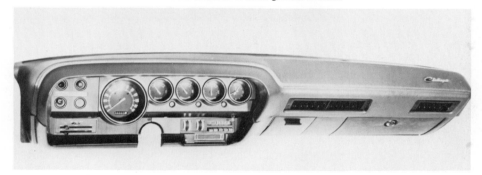

The sculpted interior panel of the 1970 Challenger was Dodge styling at its peak. This door panel has the optional power window buttons.

seat facings. To further spruce up the interior, you could order the asymmetrically styled center console.

Dodge wasted no time coming up with performance options specifically tailored to the Challenger. The back window louver package (A-44) came with a flat-black finish and included dual color-keyed racing mirrors; but this $91.10 dealer-installed option was rarely seen on the car. A bit more prevalent was the rear spoiler, code J-81, which cost $34.80; it was really more for appearance than function. A front and rear spoiler package, code A-45, included a split, two-piece flat-black front spoiler for an extra $20.85. The shaker hood scoop, code N-96, came in red to match red Challengers or black for all other body colors. This $97.30 option was at first only available on 440 Six-Pack and Hemi Challenger R/T's, but was later

The 1970 Challenger was available with either a bumblebee stripe like this or a longitudinal stripe, optional at no extra cost.

Details such as these made the Challenger a successful entry in the lucrative youth market.

offered on the 340, 383 and 440 four-barrel V-8's. This scoop fed cool air directly to the air cleaner. According to Chrysler's Larry Shepard, "Some of the Challengers with 340, 383, 440 and Hemi engines also used the 1970 T/A fiberglass hood in 1970. This was caused by a production shortage of the shakers so that the T/A fiberglass hood was used in place of the shaker on the engines with the fresh-air option. In 1971 they only used the shaker."

Incidentally, you couldn't order air conditioning with the 426 Hemi, the 440 Six-Pack or four-barrel 440 with manual transmission, or some performance axle ratios.

Road Test magazine tested a Hemi Challenger in 1970. The Hemi option, which included related heavy-duty pieces, added $1,227.50 to the

The Challenger SE (for special edition) came with an overhead consolette with three warning lights for door ajar, low fuel and seat belts.

The Challenger R/T convertible, shown with the standard performance hood, was offered only in 1970 and 1971.

base list price of the Challenger. Said *Road Test:* "In return you get power that can rattle dishes in the kitchen when you start it up in the driveway, extra attention in any service station, respect from owners of 428 Fords and SS427 Chevies, a measurable bonus in pride of ownership and immediate status as *the* car expert on your block." In addition, stated the magazine, you got ". . . insurance and operating costs matched by no other U. S.

Actor Joe Higgins played a watchful sheriff in a number of clever Dodge TV commercials in 1970. Here, racer Bobby Isaac accepts the keys to a new Challenger R/T from Higgins after winning the Texas 500 stock car race.

The standard interior of the 1970 Challenger R/T hardtop and convertible was an outstanding performance styling statement. Note the pistol grip four-speed shifter.

Dean Jeffries Automotive, Inc., offered a one-piece fiberglass front spoiler for $49 that you could bolt to your 1970 or 1971 Challenger. The spoiler is shown here installed on a 1970 Challenger T/A.

nameplate except maybe a Hemi Plymouth and the certainty that no fuzz will let you pass by unnoticed." On the strip, the Hemi Challenger covered the quarter mile in fourteen seconds at 104 mph in street trim. Around town, mileage was a mind-blowing 6.5 mpg, with 12 mpg on the highway. *Road Test* was critical of the Hemi Challenger with regard to handling and ride, but the car was conceived and marketed as a street/strip machine.

One of the rarest and wildest production Challengers you could buy was the 1970 Challenger T/A. Like the Plymouth AAR 'Cuda, the Challenger T/A was the result of a minimum production requirement of 2,500 units as dictated by the SCCA for its Trans-Am road racing series. It was designed by Chrysler's Pete Hutchinson and built by Ray Chaldwell's Autodynamics to race against the Ford Boss 302, Chevy Z-28, American Motors Javelin and other ponycars. Sam Posey drove the car to fourth place during the 1970 SCCA Trans-Am season. Powering the car was a destroked 340- to 305-ci engine, from which Chrysler's road racing team manager Pete Hutchinson managed to get 440 hp.

This Challenger T/A prototype shows the fabulous hood scoop and side exhaust. Missing on this prototype were the 340 Six-Pack graphics, which were later added to the production model.

The street version was visually identical to the racing car and it had the credentials to back it up. The 340-ci V-8 came with three two-barrel Holley carburetors on a Chrysler-designed Edelbrock aluminum intake manifold. The racing engine was limited to a single four-barrel carburetor by the SCCA. Feeding air to the production T/A's three carburetors was the most obvious yet stylish hood scoop ever seen on a Mopar. The scoop was patterned after a scoop on a pursuit plane! The one-piece fiberglass scoop and hood was painted matte-black and secured by hood pins. The Challenger T/A brochure said this hood, code N-94, was optional, but the standard steel hood with power bulge would be available later. In truth, the fiberglass hood became standard, and all T/A's built used this hood. The duck-tail-type rear spoiler was standard. A front spoiler, code J78, was optional.

The T/A had a pronounced rake for several reasons: It had E60x15 Goodyear tires in front and G60x15 tires in the rear. To clear the rear tires and provide clearance for the side exhausts, rear spring camber was increased. The suspension had front and rear antisway bars and heavy-duty shock absorbers. You chose between the four-speed manual and Torque-Flight automatic transmissions. A 3.55:1 Sure-Grip differential was standard; a 3.90:1 ratio was optional. The standard disc/drum brakes came with semimetallic brake pads for better stopping power. The car came in a choice of colors with black side stripe and block-letter T/A and 340 Six-Pack identification.

The Challenger T/A's performance was 0-60 mph in 6.0 seconds, 0-100 mph in 14.0 seconds and the quarter mile in 14.5 seconds.

Dodge advertised the T/A in the October 1970 *Hot Rod* as part of an eight-page ad for the 1971 Scat Pack. However, the 1971 T/A was never

This 1971 Challenger R/T 440 Six-Pack was the last of a powerful breed. Note the bogus rear quarter panel scoops.

released for production, due to Chrysler's decision to drop out of Trans-Am competition at the end of 1970.

Total Challenger production in 1970 came to 42,625 units.

The Challenger was a natural for drag racing. Dick Landy and the Ramchargers were just two highly visible entries on major drag strips, but major wins were not plentiful.

The biggest news from Scat City in 1971 was decompression. The majority of Chrysler's ten engines for the 1971 Challenger got lower compression ratios to run on low-lead gasoline, as decreed by the EPA. In the case of the Challenger R/T, the standard 383 Magnum V-8's compression ratio was lowered from 9.5:1 to 8.5:1. The drop in engine performance was slight.

There was pressure on the auto industry to publish more realistic horsepower ratings. This meant taking readings with the engine installed in the car with all accessories, as opposed to measuring gross flywheel horsepower. For 1971, the 383 Magnum's net horsepower was 250 compared to the previous year's 335-hp gross rating.

The rest of the Scat Pack's big V-8's—the 440 Magnum, 440 Six-Pack and the 426 Hemi—did not suffer reduced compression ratios. All had high-compression ratios requiring premium fuel, which was still available. All suspension and performance axle ratios were carried over.

The major aesthetic change to the Challenger was to the grille, with two distinct openings that altered the car's looks dramatically. On the R/T, the lower portion of the grille was blacked out and blended into the bumper, which was color-keyed. The rear bumper had the same treatment. R/T identification appeared in large black letters on the hood and the sides of the car, stopping just below the rear quarter windows with the letters R/T. Two bogus scoops in front of the rear wheel openings also identified this Challenger R/T as a 1971 model.

Model availability was juggled for 1971. The R/T SE and R/T convertible were dropped that year. Added was a base two-door coupe with fixed rear windows and a lower price tag than the hardtop. Base price for the two-door coupe was $2,727. The two-door hardtop cost $2,848. The convertible listed for $3,105. The R/T two-door hardtop listed for $3,273. Buyers could compensate for the loss of the R/T convertible by ordering one of the optional big-block engines.

Inside, the Challenger remained virtually unchanged. Simulated wood-grain inserts were added to the doors to accent the simulated wood grain already on the dash. The vinyl pleats of the bucket seats were different for 1971.

The dash on the 1972 Challenger with the Rallye Cluster option offered full instrumentation. Speedometer read to 150 mph.

127

Dodge knew that with upcoming emissions and safety standards, all-out performance cars like the Challenger R/T were threatened, but it didn't let on. "We could have saved the cars with good, aggressive management," said Chrysler's Larry Shepard. "The whole industry was to blame for being intimidated by the federal government and the insurance companies."

In the 1971 Scat Pack brochure, the Mopar enthusiast was urged to join the Dodge Scat Pack Club. For only $5.95, membership included: (1) an illustrated tune-up tips folder, (2) a Hustle Stuff parts catalog, (3) a Pocket Pack, all-weather racing jacket, (4) an official club blazer patch, (5) a "Scat Packers Unite!" bumper sticker, (6) an official club identifier folder with four pages of Dodge Scat Pack Club accessories, (7) a Dodge Scat Pack outside/inside car decal, (8) a wallet-size membership card, (9) *Scat Speaks,* an illustrated quarterly featuring club news, service and tuning tips and other articles and features, (10) a 1971 Auto Racing Guide and, finally, (11) *Dodge Performance News,* a monthly four-page flier about Dodge racing activity across the country. A Scat Pack Club membership was a bargain, to be sure.

Challenger production dropped to 28,901 in 1971. The dramatic drop was attributed to insurance rates that made it prohibitively expensive to insure the high-performance Challengers. The figures coming in to Chrysler showed the majority of Challengers sold in 1971 were equipped with smaller-displacement engines. For this and other reasons, the 383, 440 Six-Pack and 426 Hemi were dropped for 1972.

Only two Challenger models were available for 1972. The Challenger two-door hardtop listed for $2,790. The other model available was the Chal-

The four-barrel 340 V-8 was the largest engine you could order in the 1972 Challenger Rallye. The big-block engines were no longer available, and the Challenger convertible was history, as well. Styling remained unchanged for 1973 and 1974.

lenger two-door Rallye hardtop, which listed for $3,082. The back cover blurb for the 1972 Challenger Rallye reflected the new market reality: "The way things are today, maybe what you need is not the world's hottest car. Maybe what you need is a well-balanced, thoroughly instrumented road machine. One with a highly individualized style; a well-proportioned balance between acceleration, road-holding, braking—you know the bit.

"This is it. Challenger Rallye. Reasonable to buy, to run. About as enjoyable in the legal range as anything its size. And a lot more thoughtfully done."

The Challenger Rallye came with a 240-hp four-barrel 340 V-8, three-on-the-floor synchromesh manual transmission, 3.23:1 axle ratio, performance hood with scoops, and dual exhausts with bright tips. Performance could be increased by ordering the optional four-speed manual transmission and the Performance Axle Package, which came with 3.55:1 heavy-duty axle, Sure-Grip differential, high-performance radiator, fan shroud and—when power steering was ordered—a power-steering oil cooler.

Appearancewise, the 1972 Challenger got a new grille. The Challenger Rallye came with simulated side body louvers with black tape stripes aligned with the louvers. The ever-handsome Rallye wheels were mounted

The body style of the Dodge Challenger remained unchanged during its five years of production between 1970 and 1974. Over 100,000 units were built during that time but few remain today. This is a 1973.

with F70x14 Goodyear tires. Only two High-Impact colors were available to make the '72 Challenger stand out: Hemi Orange and Top Banana.

The Challenger Rallye actually was not a bad package. It *was* a better-balanced, better-handling all-around machine, and served the purposes of the majority of Challenger buyers looking for something more than the plain Challenger. If the Dodge enthusiast was looking for something more in the way of straight-line acceleration, he had to look to the bigger-bodied Charger.

Total Challenger production for 1972 dropped only slightly from 1971: 27,770 units were sold in the Challenger's third year of production.

The 1973 Challengers were carry-over models, virtually identical to 1972 models. The only discernible difference was slightly larger bumper pads on the front and rear bumpers for added protection. The Rallye was no longer a standard model but now an option and its power was down-graded to a 318-ci V-8, although the 240-hp 340 V-8 was optional. The Performance Axle Package was also still available. Curiously, sales jumped to 30,221 in 1973.

The Challenger entered its fifth year of production in 1974. There were some minor improvements. The bumpers were strengthened to withstand 5 mph impacts, yet still looked good. The 340 V-8 was dropped for a 245-hp 360-ci V-8. The Rallye and Performance Axle Package options were again offered.

The Chrysler Corporation abruptly decided to cease production of the Dodge Challenger only a few months into the model year. Only 6,063 Challengers were built and sold in 1974.

Over 135,000 Challengers were built during its five-year production run. Catching sight of a Challenger on the road today, however, is rare. You can usually find the greatest concentration of Dodge E-bodies at major AHRA and NHRA meets around the country, as well as at various Mopar club meets.

Challengers are still popular on the quarter-mile strip. This 426 Hemi Challenger was campaigned by Vaughn Currie and Tom Hutton.

CHAPTER TEN

Road Runner And GTX
1970-1974

When Plymouth announced the Rapid Transit System for 1970, it generated a lot of excitement among enthusiasts in general and Mopar nuts in particular. Virtually every American car manufacturer was offering performance cars in various sizes and stages of performance and hawking their cars using a "top this" type of advertising. Selection was so great, it was difficult for a buyer to make a decision.

In an effort to rise above all the performance hoopla from other car companies and draw attention to its product line, Plymouth created the Rapid Transit System. As stated earlier, the System was not just a fleet of cars but a whole support network between Plymouth and its performance car buyers. While some manufacturers imitated Plymouth's approach, none offered such a comprehensive package.

The Belvedere-based Road Runner and Satellite-based GTX were reskinned for 1970. They shared the same 116-inch wheelbase and body as before, differing in trim and power train offerings. The body received mild but noticeable refinement. The sharp creases that were previously along the fender flanks were shaved off. A nonfunctional scoop was sculpted into the sides between the rear wheels and the door. The hood received a prominent power bulge; the dual hood scoops of before were gone. The front and rear ends were redesigned as well. Although the roofline remained unchanged, the reworking of the sheetmetal gave the car a completely new look. The result was the best-looking Road Runner and GTX to date.

The Road Runner was again offered as a two-door coupe for $2,896, a two-door hardtop for $3,034 and a two-door convertible for $3,289.

The standard Road Runner four-barrel 383 V-8 still pumped out 335 hp, but compression ratio was dropped from 10.0:1 to 9.5:1. Plymouth switched from a Carter four-barrel carburetor to a Holley four-barrel carburetor. A heavy-duty three-speed manual transmission with floor shifter was now standard and the heavy-duty four-speed manual transmission was made optional. The superb TorqueFlight automatic transmission was, of course, optional also.

The two optional engines on the 1970 Road Runner were the 375-hp 440 6-bbl and the 425-hp 426 Hemi. The 440 6-bbl V-8 still ran a 10.5:1 compression ratio. It had the same high-lift, long-duration, high-overlap camshaft used in the 335-hp 383. Intake duration was 276 degrees, exhaust duration was 292 degrees and overlap was fifty-four degrees. The 335-hp 383 used the same cylinder heads as the 440 6-bbl, so the intake valve diameter of 2.08 inches and exhaust valve diameter of 1.74 inches were the same also. The 440 6-bbl had the distinction of using three Holley two-barrel carburetors.

The fiberglass hood with mammoth scoop used on the 1969 440 6-bbl Road Runner was gone for 1970. In its place was a redesigned Air Grabber system optional on the 440 6-bbl for 1970. An electric solenoid switch inside the car operated the vacuum-actuated trap door in the center of the hood's power bulge to raise or lower the Air Grabber. This design did away with the restrictive and cumbersome system used before. The 1970 Air Grabber forced cool outside air directly to the air cleaner. It also provided the ultimate form of intimidation at stoplights. If the 440 6-bbl decal on the side of the power bulge wasn't enough to shake up the driver of the GTO next to you, a flip of the switch popped up the Air Grabber with its menacing graphics. That was usually enough to crumble the confidence of most street racers. Plymouth stated the new Air Grabber was good for knocking a tenth of a second off your quarter-mile elapsed time, and added approximately 1.5 mph to your trap speed.

The optional 426 Hemi's specifications remained unchanged for 1970 except for one important modification. The mechanical lifters were replaced by hydraulic lifters. This reduced the frequency of tuneups and allowed Chrysler to better control emissions. The Hemi still ran a 10.25:1 compression ratio. Camshaft timing was the most radical of all of Chrysler's engines. Intake and exhaust duration were both 292 degrees. Overlap was sixty-eight degrees. The intake valve diameter of 2.25 inches and exhaust valve diameter of 1.94 inches remained the same since its introduction in the 1964 race Hemi and the 1966 street Hemi. Two Carter four-barrel carburetors contributed to the Hemi's conservative rating of 425 hp. The cast

The Road Runner and GTX received new bodies for 1970. This Road Runner is equipped with the 440+6 V-8 having three two-barrel carburetors, and the Air Grabber hood scoop.

132

iron headers on the Hemi were superior to those on the 440 V-8's but both engines employed 2½-inch exhaust pipes and tail pipes with huge reverse-flow canister mufflers. The 426 Hemi came standard with the Air Grabber, whether it was ordered in the Road Runner or GTX.

Plymouth also published specific rear axle ratio availability in 1970. The back of the Rapid Transit System brochure showed a chart to help buyers pick the ratio they wanted. Plymouth called these "Supergears for Plymouth Supercars."

The Road Runner came standard with a 3.23:1 axle ratio in both manual- and automatic-transmission-equipped cars. With the optional 3.55:1 or 3.91:1 ratios, you also got a Sure-Grip differential. All these axles used Chrysler's heavy-duty 8¾-inch-diameter ring gear.

When you ordered either the 440 6-bbl or the 426 Hemi, Chrysler made sure you got driveline insurance. The 3.23:1 ratio was standard only with the TorqueFlight automatic transmission with these engines; an optional ratio of 3.55:1 with Sure-Grip could be ordered. When you ordered

As this promotional photograph proved, Plymouth didn't take the Road Runner too seriously. This 1970 model was powered by a 440 6-bbl V-8 with Air Grabber hood scoop.

the four-speed manual transmission, you got as part of the package a 3.54:1 rear axle ratio with Sure-Grip. A 4.10:1 ratio with Sure-Grip was also optional in either four-speed- or automatic-transmission-equipped Road Runners using these big engines. Regardless of rear axle ratio, when you ordered the 440 6-bbl or the 426 Hemi, you got the Dana-built model 60 9¾-inch-diameter extra-heavy-duty ring gearset to withstand the awesome torque of these engines.

In its Rapid Transit System brochure, Plymouth also released suspension specifications for all its performance cars. The Road Runner's standard front torsion bars measured 0.90 inch in diameter having a spring rate of 113 pounds per inch. The heavy-duty rear leaf springs with 4½ leaves on the left and right had a spring rate of 129 pounds per inch. The front stabilizer bar measured 0.94 inch in diameter. There was no rear stabilizer bar. The shock absorbers were heavy-duty.

When you ordered the 440 6-bbl or 426 Hemi engine, the suspension was beefed up accordingly. The extra-heavy-duty front torsion bars measured 0.92 inch in diameter with a spring rate of 124 pounds per inch. The extra-heavy-duty rear suspension used five leaves plus two half-leaves on the left and six leaves on the right, with a spring rate of 148 pounds per inch. The front stabilizer bar diameter was the same as that on the 383 V-8 Road Runner. The shock absorbers were extra-heavy-duty.

No less important to the 1970 Road Runner buyer—after choosing the engine, transmission and axle ratio—was the selection of comfort and appearance options. If the bench front seat was too plain for your tastes then you could order the newly designed contoured bucket seats. The 8000 rpm tachometer was practically a must in a car like the Road Runner, and it was cheap insurance for knowing when to upshift; the redline started at 5000 rpm. Wire wheel covers were available with the standard fourteen-

A 1970 Plymouth GTX and Road Runner pose for their portrait on a dry lake bed. This GTX was powered by a 6-bbl 440 V-8 with Air Grabber hood scoop.

inch wheel. The 14x5½-inch chromed steel road wheel was optional on 383 and 440 Road Runners. The Rallye wheel, with the holes running around the perimeter of the wheel reflected in the trim ring, was a new option offered in 14x5½-inch and 15x7-inch dimensions depending on the engine chosen. These wheels were also part of the optional heavy-duty suspension package for standard Belvederes.

Paint and graphics options were abundant in 1970. You could order your Road Runner in one of eighteen exterior colors, and top it off with a vinyl roof. There was new flat-black hood striping to set off the power bulge. You could even order Road Runner decals for the sides of the car showing the swift bird leaving a dust trail from the bogus scoop on the sides of the car all the way to the front of the car.

Plymouth targeted the 1970 GTX at the twenty-five-year-olds and up, as before. This group made more money and could afford and appreciate the GTX's more luxurious fittings while still getting the solid kick-in-the-pants the 375-hp four-barrel 440 V-8 could provide. List price for the 1970 GTX hardtop was $3,535. The GTX convertible was dropped.

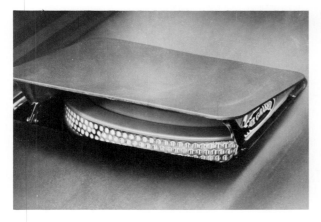

The Air Grabber hood scoop available on the 1970 Road Runner and GTX gave a straight shot of cool air directly to the air cleaner.

The 1970 GTX offered more power and luxury than the Road Runner and was aimed at the executive hot rodder.

The four-barrel 440 suffered a slight compression ratio drop in 1970, from 10.1:1 to 9.7:1. Horsepower and torque ratings were the same, however. Except for the differences in the induction system and compression ratio, the four-barrel 440 used in the GTX had the same mechanicals and specifications as the optionally available 440 6-bbl, except for the lifters and cam drive. The 426 Hemi was also optional in the GTX. The Air Grabber was optional with either 440 engine and standard on the 426 Hemi.

The heavy-duty TorqueFlight automatic transmission was standard, with the heavy-duty four-speed manual transmission optional.

The GTX came standard with a rear axle ratio of 3.23:1. Optional ratios available were the same as those offered in the Road Runner with the optional engines and transmissions.

Regardless of the engine you chose to power your GTX, the car came standard with the extra-heavy-duty suspension as used in Road Runners with the 440 6-bbl or 426 Hemi engines.

The GTX shared options with the Road Runner that were not already standard. And with virtually the same weight and mechanical specifications the 1970 Road Runner and GTX were really no faster than earlier models. However, there was one way to go *faster* in the Road Runner line: the limited production 1970 Superbird.

In the late sixties, Plymouth was offered the opportunity to build a highly aerodynamic car for NASCAR racing. At the time, Plymouth had Richard Petty—the most successful driver on the Grand National circuit—and didn't see the need for such a car. Dodge accepted the challenge and the 1969 Charger Daytona was the result. When Petty left Plymouth and its boxy Belvedere to race the more aerodynamic Ford Torino for the 1969 racing season, Plymouth realized its mistake in not upgrading the Belvedere aerodynamically. In an effort to get Petty back, Plymouth set to work.

The Dodge Charger Daytona broke much new ground in the field of automotive aerodynamics. Plymouth had access to this information, making the job of streamlining the Belvedere much easier and faster. The result of wind tunnel testing produced a car similar to the Daytona in appearance; but it was not identical.

This decal on the vertical stabilizers of the Superbird told nonautomotive types what car they were gawking at.

A smaller decal was affixed to the Superbird nose cone.

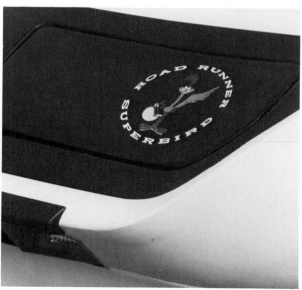

Plymouth used a preproduction 1970 Belvedere as the basis of its efforts. In keeping with the performance image, the production version would be sold as the ultimate Road Runner—a Superbird.

The front fenders of the Belvedere did not lend themselves well to adopting a fiberglass nose cone. Plymouth replaced the fenders with those from the 1970 Dodge Coronet. There was a hood/nose cone mismatch, so a plug was fashioned to provide a reasonably smooth transition. The nose cone on the Superbird was not interchangeable with the one used on the Daytona. The rear backlight was a specially molded convex piece with a plug below it to allow a smooth transition to the rear deck. Unlike the Dodge Charger 500 and Daytona, the Superbird came with a mandatory vinyl roof in order to save on the cost of hand finishing the bodywork. The rear uprights supporting the horizontal stabilizer were unique to the Superbird also, being slightly more swept back than those on the Daytona. The Superbird also came with a front spoiler and fender scoops. The latter weren't functional; they were merely bolted onto the tops of the fenders; on the racing Superbirds, these provided tire clearance. Racing-style hood pins were standard.

Creative Industries—the same firm that produced the Charger 500 and Daytona—also handled the 2,000 Superbirds required by NASCAR rules to qualify as production cars.

Despite the Superbird's limited production, buyers had a choice of three engines. The 375-hp four-barrel 440 V-8 used in the GTX was standard in the Superbird. The 390-hp 440 6-bbl or the 425-hp 426 Hemi were optional.

The 1970 Road Runner Superbird came standard with the four-barrel 440 V-8. The 440+6 and the 426 Hemi were optional. The Air Grabber hood scoop was not available on the Superbird.

For transmissions, you could choose the TorqueFlight automatic, which included the Performance Axle Package, or the four-speed manual which included the Trak Pak.

The car rode on F70x14-inch Goodyear wide-profile tires. F60x15-inch Goodyear extra-wide tires were optional. In either case, the Rallye wheels were standard. Power steering and power front disc brakes were also standard.

You could order your Superbird in Alpine White, Vitamin C Orange, Lemon Twist, Lime Light, Blue Fire Metallic, Tor-Red or Corporation Blue. Superbird decals were affixed to the sides of the vertical stabilizers. A smaller, similar decal was affixed to the left concealed headlight. The top of the nose cone was set off by two large, flat-black paint patches.

Inside, you had a choice of either black or white vinyl seats. The front bucket seats could be ordered in place of the standard bench seat.

The reverse-facing front fender scoops on the production Superbird were for show only.

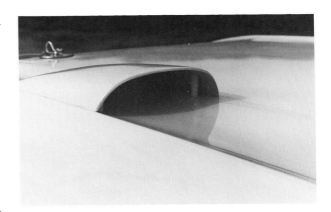

Richard Petty returned to Plymouth for 1970, but lost the Grand National title to Bobby Isaac in a Dodge Daytona.

Just how fast could the production Superbird go? That was determined by the engine and rear axle chosen. More than a few drivers saw their Superbirds exceed 140 mph on long, clear stretches of road, and with the Hemi, top speed was much higher.

With the Superbird, Plymouth did succeed in drawing Richard Petty back to Plymouth. For the 1970 NASCAR season, however, Petty was up against a formidable field of veteran drivers, many behind the wheels of Dodge Daytonas. When the dust settled at the end of the season, Petty had won five of the eight Grand National races in which Superbirds got the checkered flag. The Championship, however, went to Bobby Isaac in a Dodge Daytona.

Sales of the GTX and Road Runner dropped fifty percent from 1969 levels. It was the same story of the insurance industry cracking down on such cars with surcharges, which made it difficult to own a muscle car. Road Runner sales were respectable at 41,484 units, but this was a far cry from the year before. GTX sales totaled only 7,740 units.

There were many changes to the Rapid Transit System in 1971. The Belvedere name was dropped and Satellite formed the basis of Plymouth's intermediate line. The two-door lineup included Satellite Coupe, Satellite, Road Runner, Satellite Custom, Satellite Sebring, Satellite Brougham, Satellite Regent, Satellite Sebring Plus and GTX, in ascending order of price. None of these cars was offered as a convertible. Chrysler planned to withdraw from NASCAR competition in 1971, so the Superbird was not offered again.

Along with a new name, Plymouth gave its intermediate a completely new body. Contours were softer, more rounded—what Plymouth referred to in its brochure as "fuselage" styling. The Satellite had pronounced wheelwell bulges, which gave the Road Runner and GTX a particularly muscular look. A new performance hood had outward-facing simulated

This clever advertising photo of the 1971 Road Runner drew smiles from owners and nonowners alike.

vents which announced engine displacement—either 383, 440, 400+6 or Hemi, depending on the standard or optional engine. Wheelbase was now 115 inches. Rear track was increased three inches to sixty-two inches. This improved the car's stability and handling.

The Road Runner was only available as a hardtop in 1971. Its list price was $3,147. The standard four-barrel 383 was now rated at 300 gross hp. The loss of thirty-five horsepower was due to a drop in compression ratio, now 8.5:1, taking the horsepower reading at 4800 rpm instead of 5200 rpm, and less radical camshaft timing. Plymouth also published net horsepower for the Road Runner 383, which was 250 hp at 4800 rpm. All other specifications regarding transmissions, rear axle ratio and suspension remained the same.

The six-barrel 440 and the eight-barrel 426 Hemi were still optional in the Road Runner. On specification charts and as displayed graphically on the car, the six-barrel 440 appeared as "440+6." For 1971, the 440+6 was detuned slightly. Compression ratio dropped slightly from 10.5:1 to 10.3:1. Intake was 268 degrees, exhaust was 284 degrees and overlap was forty-six degrees. This same camshaft was used in the four-barrel 383 and the four-barrel 440 for high-performance applications. Gross horsepower dropped only five horsepower to 385. The net rating was 330 hp.

Even the street Hemi, now in its sixth and last year of production, didn't escape emissions modifications. Compression ratio was reduced to 10.2:1. It was still rated at 425 gross hp, with a net rating of 350 hp and it was still an awesome engine.

Road Runners and GTX's with the 440+6 or 426 Hemi engine bound for California came with silenced air cleaners to conform to that state's strict drive-by noise standards.

There was a host of new options for the 1971 Road Runner. A rear spoiler was available on the bird for the first time. The 1971 Rapid Transit System brochure showed a Road Runner illustration with two outboard

Very few Road Runners with the 440+6 V-8 were built in 1971. It was the last year you could order this engine or the 426 Hemi.

front spoilers, but these were not mentioned as a possible option. To complement the black rear spoiler, new backlight louvers, similar to those offered on the 'Cuda, could also be ordered. Also new for '71 were reflective strobe stripes that ran from the rear wheelwells up to and over the roof. An optional elastomeric color-keyed front bumper gave the car a purposeful look. Inside, the optional contour bucket seats were offered in a number of color combinations, the most striking being black seats with orange inserts.

The Air Grabber was still available and worked the same way as the year before, but for 1971 it came with a new performance hood with a prominent power bulge. Road Runners equipped with the Air Grabber that year are extremely rare today.

The 1971 GTX, with a list price of $3,733 held up the executive branch of the Rapid Transit System. Its standard four-barrel 440 lost only five horsepower to emission controls. Its gross rating of 370 hp worked out to a net rating of 305 hp. The 440+6 and 426 Hemi were optional. The GTX was available with all the same options as the Road Runner, except those that came standard.

Sales for the Road Runner and GTX dropped even further in 1971. Only 14,484 Road Runners were sold that year, a far cry from the soaring sales of 1969. The GTX fared even worse; a mere 3,212 units left Chrysler-

The 1971 Road Runner and GTX were available with a striking two-tone bucket seat option.

The last year Richard Petty was officially sponsored by Plymouth was 1971.

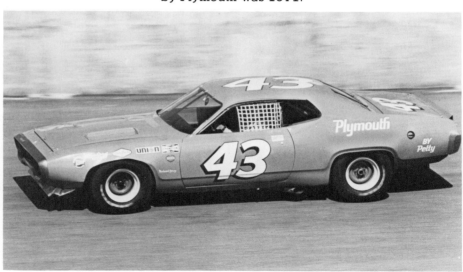

Plymouth dealerships in 1971. This convinced Plymouth to drop the GTX model that year.

Despite poor sales, Plymouth's E-body, with the help of Richard Petty, performed brilliantly on the Grand National stock car circuit. Petty won his third Championship and a total of $333,148.

With the introduction of Plymouth's 1972 models, the bell was clearly tolling for the Rapid Transit System. The GTX was gone, leaving only the Road Runner hardtop for $3,095 to hold down Plymouth's mid-size performance offering. It still came standard with the three-speed manual transmission, heavy-duty suspension and brakes, front and rear stabilizer bars and F70x14 tires. The standard engine was the four-barrel 383 bored out to 400 cubic inches. Compression ratio was lowered even further to 8.2:1. It was rated at 255 hp, net.

Performancewise, help was available. A GTX package option was offered which included a 280 hp four-barrel 440. When this engine was ordered, special designations appeared on the sides of the car and the trunk lid. The Air Grabber was still available, except in California. The brochure for the 1972 Satellite listed the availability of the six-barrel 440 with 10.3:1 compression ratio (except in California, again) but according to Chrysler staff engineer Larry Shepard, this engine was dropped from the 1972 lineup because it did not pass Environmental Protection Agency certification and could not be sold.

It is interesting to note that Plymouth published both gross and net horsepower figures in its 1971 Satellite brochure but released no horsepower figures at all in its 1972 Satellite brochure.

Other performance options relevant to Road Runner buyers included a choice between the four-speed manual or TorqueFlight automatic transmissions. Although not specifically mentioned in the 1972 brochure, apparently there was a Performance Axle Package which included a higher numerical axle ratio than the 3.23:1 ratio that came standard. Choosing from several optional ratios, however, was a thing of the past. To improve traction with the bigger engine, the Sure-Grip differential was available.

There were minor cosmetic changes made to the 1972 Road Runner. A new front grille distinguished it from the '71. With the standard performance hood, you could order the new hood and fender tape stripes. If the Air Grabber was ordered, a different hood and deck tape treatment could be ordered to dress up your otherwise unobtrusive Road Runner. The reflective roof tape stripe was again optional.

You could get your bird in one of sixteen colors but there were fewer eye-popping colors to make it stand out. The standard bench seat and

The Rallye Instrument Cluster was standard in all 1971-74 Road Runners and GTX's. Early designs had a silver finish; later designs used simulated wood grain.

interior were offered in blue, green and black. An optional bench seat with adjustable head restraints was offered in blue, green, tan, gold and white with black. The handsome, optional pleated bucket seats and matching interior came in blue, green, gold, black and white with black. The striking color combinations for the bucket seats offered the year before were not available in '72. Vinyl roofs, either full or canopy style, were available in black, white, green and gold.

Although Plymouth was no longer officially involved in NASCAR, Richard Petty carried the Plymouth name to glory. With Andy Granatelli's STP sponsorship, Petty streaked to his fourth Grand National title in 1972.

When the 1973 Road Runner made its appearance, a good number of its feathers had been plucked. For starters, the '73 Satellite received all-new front end sheetmetal. The chrome loop front bumper of the previous two years was gone, replaced by a more traditional bumper designed to withstand a 5 mph fixed-barrier impact. Structurally, all Satellites for '73 featured isolated front and rear suspensions, designed to give a less harsh, quieter ride. There were rubber bushings and isolators at all points between the suspension and body. The cross-member alone was separated from the body by six rubber isolators. This adversely affected the Road Runner's taut handling characteristics.

The big shocker came from the '73 Road Runner's engine compartment. The standard engine was now a two-barrel 318 V-8 producing 170 hp. For all 318 V-8-equipped Plymouths, the muffler used was retuned to

This 1972 Road Runner is shown with optional hood and fender tape stripes and canopy vinyl roof.

reduce engine noise. Plymouth probably went to a standard 318 in the Road Runner for 1973 to keep the list price down to $3,115.

Fortunately, there were three optional engines. You could choose from the 240-hp four-barrel 340, the 255-hp four-barrel 400 or the 280-hp four-barrel 440. The 400 V-8 was not available with the California emissions package; thus this engine was simply not available to California Road Runner buyers. The Air Grabber was no longer available on the Road Runner.

The '73 Road Runner still came with heavy-duty springs and front and rear stabilizer bars, but heavy-duty shock absorbers were optional.

The standard heavy-duty three-speed manual transmission could be replaced by the four-speed manual transmission on all engines except the 440. The optional TorqueFlight automatic transmission was available with all V-8's. With the standard 318, Plymouth used a smaller 8¼-inch ring gear with a 3.21 axle ratio. A Performance Axle Package was optional only with the Road Runner in the Satellite line, but Plymouth did not specify the axle ratio. The Sure-Grip differential was classified as a "comfort/convenience" option, not a performance option.

Inside, the '73 interior was all new. The standard vinyl bench seat came in blue, green or black. The optional bench seat, as part of a Decor Package offered only in the Road Runner, came in blue, green, parchment, black or gold. Finally, the newly designed bucket seats were offered in blue, green, parchment, black, white or gold.

Outside, there were sixteen standard colors and only one optional color to choose from. The Road Runner came with the body side and roof "strobe" tape stripe as well as specific Road Runner trim and ornamentation. A color-matching hood tape treatment could make the performance hood bulge stand out.

The 1973 Road Runner was underpowered with the standard 318 V-8. The 1974 model was visually identical.

Except for replacing the optional four-barrel 340 with a new four-barrel 360 V-8, a subtle grille change and a new selection of exterior colors and interior seating, the 1974 Road Runner was a carry-over from 1973. List price was $3,444. By now, many of the features that at first had been standard—the big V-8, the four-speed manual transmission and the heavy-duty suspension—were now all extra-cost options. The Road Runner could still be made into a good performer with the right options, but it had strayed from its original concept of offering the most bang for the buck.

While the forces that affected the Road Runner affected all performance cars, it was nevertheless sad to see this charismatic car reduced to a caricature of its former self, even if the horn still did go "Beep-Beep!"

CHAPTER ELEVEN

Mighty Mini-Mopars 1970-1974

As the seventies opened, Dodge and Plymouth reevaluated the place their compacts held in the Chrysler Corporation performance lineup. Dodge decided to deemphasize brute acceleration by dropping the 383 and 440 GTS—the latter admittedly for the drag strip only—in favor of compacts having a more acceptable power-to-weight ratio. Plymouth finally decided to market a performance compact, after watching Dodge snare a significant market share with its Dart GTS.

Dodge considerably reduced the number of compact performance offerings for 1970. The GT two-door hardtop and convertible as well as the GTS two-door hardtop and convertible were dropped. Only the Swinger two-door hardtop for $2,261 and the Swinger 340 two-door hardtop for $2,631 were carried over from 1969. The good news was that both models were roughly $200 cheaper than the year before.

Stylistically, the 1970 Swinger was unchanged from 1969 except for minor cosmetic changes. It still rode on a 111-inch wheelbase with a 57.4-inch front track and a 55.6-inch rear track.

Naturally, the Swinger 340 was of interest to Dodge performance buffs on limited budgets. There were some changes to the Swinger 340's standard equipment for 1970. Dodge achieved a lower price by using a fully synchronized three-speed manual transmission with floor shifter. The four-speed manual transmission was now optional. The Swinger 340 was the only car in the 1970 Scat Pack to have front disc brakes standard.

In its 1970 performance brochure, *Big News from Scat City,* Dodge stated that the four-barrel 340 V-8 in the Swinger 340 came with an 8.8:1 compression ratio. This was probably a printing error because the engine was still rated at 275 hp and still required premium fuel. Other sources listed the engine as having a 10.5:1 compression ratio, and Plymouth's equivalent engine did have a 10.5:1 compression ratio.

The 1970 Swinger 340 came with nonfunctional hood scoops with 340 on their sides. These scoops were the same as used on the Coronet Super Bee when the Ramcharger fresh-air performance hood was ordered, but the Ramcharger was not optional on the Swinger 340.

Rounding out the Swinger 340's list of standard items were Rallye suspension, a 3.23:1 rear axle ratio, E70x14 fiberglass-belted bias-ply tires mounted to 14x5.5J steel wheels, a bumblebee stripe and bright chrome tip exhaust.

The option list for the Swinger 340 was extensive. All-vinyl bucket seats could replace the standard bench seat, and this permitted you to order the center console. A performance hood paint treatment making the entire hood and scoops flat-black made the car look more ominous. Hood tie-down pins were a racy touch. You could add power brakes, steering and windows. Rallye wheels were a visual improvement over the standard wheelcovers, but wire wheelcovers were also optional. It was wise to order the 6000 rpm tachometer in the high-revving Swinger 340. A vinyl roof in black or white added a nice contrast to the paint color you chose. This is by no means the entire list of options available for the Swinger 340, but gives a good idea of the choices available to buyers.

Plymouth introduced a sporty new model for 1970: the Duster. The Valiant was once again the stepfather of a new addition to the Plymouth line. The same technique that spawned the 1964 Barracuda was employed for the Duster. It was designed to use the same front end sheetmetal, windshield, running gear and 108-inch wheelbase as the Valiant; but Plymouth's stylists gave the car an entirely new look by using a modified fastback configuration with a good degree of tumble-home to the side glass.

The time available to get the Duster into production was at a premium. Dick Macadam was vice president of styling at the Plymouth studio during the late seventies, and he had these comments on the new car: "It was a very late program, under extreme pressure, and needed a shot in the arm very quickly. It was sold through product planning, sales division and finally corporate management in a very short period of time—a few weeks." While most automotive designs are a team effort, the initial Duster sketches were drawn up by one person, Neal Walling, who then carried them out in clay model form.

The Duster was offered in two forms. The base Duster came standard with a choice of either the 198-ci one-barrel slant six or the 318-ci two-barrel V-8. The 225-ci one-barrel slant six was optional. List price for the base Duster coupe was $2,172. The second model was the Duster 340 powered by the 275-hp four-barrel 340 V-8. With a list price of $2,547, the Plymouth Duster 340 was the least expensive car in the Rapid Transit System.

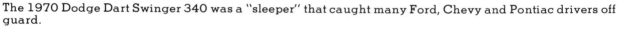

The 1970 Dodge Dart Swinger 340 was a "sleeper" that caught many Ford, Chevy and Pontiac drivers off guard.

With its relatively low weight and high-output small-block wedge V-8, the Duster had a favorable power-to-weight ratio. And Plymouth remarked on it in its Rapid Transit System brochure. "We think Supercars should be affordable," the brochure read. "Heck, what's the sense of liking anything if you have to wait until you're pushing 30 and your second million to enjoy it?

"With that in mind we set about to do an encore to Road Runner and create the industry's lowest-priced high performance car.

"Better yet, we decided to make it a sleeper that would blow the doors off hulking, pretentious behemoths twice its size.

"For a start, we needed a body shell that was strong, simple and inexpensive to produce. It also had to be lightweight and compact, so that it could achieve a Supercar power-to-weight ratio with a relatively small displacement engine. We figured that with a good driver and (optional) 3.91 gearing, it should be able to just touch the 13-second bracket. (In fact, it would *have* to; because any car that can't cut a 14-second quarter doesn't qualify for R.T.S. membership.)"

The Duster 340 was indeed a lot of car for the money. The high-performance 340 V-8 developed 275 hp at 5000 rpm and 340 pounds-feet of torque at 3200 rpm using a single Carter AVS four-barrel carburetor. The compression ratio was 10.5:1. The timing of the camshaft was 276 degrees

This medallion identified the 1970 Dodge Dart Swinger.

The styling of the 1970 Dodge Dart Swinger two-door hardtop was clean and understated.

intake, 284 degrees exhaust and fifty-two degrees of overlap; this was only slightly less radical than the camshaft in the four-barrel and six-barrel 440 V-8's.

The heavy-duty three-speed manual transmission and 3.23:1 rear axle ratio were standard. Either the heavy-duty four-speed manual transmission or high-upshift TorqueFlight automatic transmission was optional. Two optional rear axle ratios were 3.55:1 and 3.91:1, both with Sure-Grip.

As with other cars in the Rapid Transit System, the Duster 340 came with a heavy-duty suspension. The front torsion bars were 0.87 inch in diameter, with a spring rate of 106 pounds per inch. Front stabilizer bar diameter was 0.88 inch. The Duster 340 received six rear leaf springs on both left and right sides, but Plymouth didn't give their spring rates.

This was the only car in the Rapid Transit System to come with front disc brakes standard. The rear drum brakes measured 10x1¾ inches. The Duster 340 rode on E70x14 tires mounted to 14x5½-inch Rallye wheels.

"Performance alone does not a Supercar make," the Rapid Transit System brochure read, and showed an array of appearance and comfort options to prove it. The Duster 340 came standard with the Rallye wheel; the only optional wheel was the wire wheelcover. A vinyl roof in a choice of colors contrasted well with the selection of seven standard exterior colors. In place of the standard vinyl bench seat you could order a bucket-seat-and-console arrangement. The pistol-grip shifter on the optional four-speed manual transmission was a real macho touch, and you could optimize performance with an 8000 rpm tachometer. The tachometer, however, was redlined from 5000 rpm to 8000 rpm. The Rapid Transit System brochure did not give many details of the other options offered in the Duster. More information on Duster options could be found in the 1970 Duster brochure.

How did the Duster do on the drag strip in sanctioned competition? In terms of numbers, the Duster lost out to the bigger and heavier Mopars

Drag racer Tom "The Mongoose" McEwen campaigned this 1970 426 Hemi-powered Plymouth Duster funny car. Speeds over 200 mph were common.

such as the Road Runner, the GTX and the Charger. These bigger cars were more desirable in the minds of both racers and spectators because they could run the big-blocks for more speed and excitement.

For 1971, Dodge produced its own model of Plymouth's stylish Duster. Dodge's version was called the Demon. Some cited the car's name as less than appropriate. Despite this, it was perhaps a better choice than Beaver—a name Dodge management had considered and, fortunately, dropped. The Demon logo consisted of the word Demon and a devilish little character holding a pitchfork, the end of which formed the letter m in the middle of Demon. This logo—a decal—appeared on the sides of the front fenders and the taillight panel.

The Demon shared the same body shell with the Plymouth Duster. The two cars differed primarily in the grille and rear taillight assembly. An interesting manufacturing step shared by both the Demon and the Duster

In 1971, Dodge marketed the new Demon, similar to Plymouth's Duster. This one has the optional vinyl roof, cloth-and-vinyl interior and Tuff steering wheel.

This 1971 Demon 340 has the optional hood scoops and performance hood paint treatment.

was the blending-in of the taillight panel with the rear quarter panels so no seam was visible. This was done by leading, filing and sanding, and finally priming the seam so it was invisible. This was a routine operation on the roofs of cars.

There were two models: The Demon two-door coupe listed for $2,343 and came standard with a choice of either the 198-ci slant six or the 318-ci V-8. The other model was the Demon 340 two-door coupe with a list price of $2,721. The Demon was termed a coupe instead of a hardtop because the rear windows did not roll down; they were hinged to swing out about two inches to permit ventilation.

The Demon 340 replaced the Swinger 340 as Dodge's performance compact. The Swinger two-door hardtop was now merely a sportier-looking Dart, powered by a small six or 318 V-8.

The heart of the Demon 340 was its engine: the 275-hp four-barrel 340 V-8, with dual exhaust. This was backed up by Chrysler's heavy-duty three-speed manual transmission with floor shifter. The Rallye Suspension Package with heavy-duty front torsion bars, front stabilizer bar, rear springs and shock absorbers improved the car's handling. The front drum brakes measured 10x2¼ inches and the rear drum brakes measured 10x1¾ inches.

Changes to the 1971 Duster 340 were limited to a new grille and strong tape stripe graphics.

The E70x14 wide-tread bias-belted tires were mounted to 14x5.5J wheels. Inside, a vinyl front bench seat was standard, with interior colors in blue, tan or black. Instrumentation included a 150 mph speedometer. Outside, the Demon 340 was available in fourteen standard colors and four extra-cost, High-Impact colors. The optional vinyl roof was particularly effective in black or white. A body side tape stripe in black or white was standard.

There were numerous performance and performance-related options for the Demon 340. In place of the standard three-speed manual transmission you could order the heavy-duty four-speed manual transmission or the high-upshift three-speed TorqueFlight automatic transmission. Dual hood scoops and a blacked-out hood paint treatment backed up the Demon 340's performance with looks to match. Hood pins lent a racy look. A rear spoiler was available. Inside, available options included cloth-and-vinyl bench seats, vinyl bucket seats, center console, a thick-rim 14½-inch-diameter Tuff steering wheel, and a 6000 rpm tachometer.

How was the Demon 340's performance at the drag strip? With the stock 3.23:1 rear axle, 0-60 mph came in 6.5 seconds and the quarter mile was covered in 14.5 seconds. The car's power-to-weight ratio was almost identical to Dodge's bigger performance cars. The Demon 340's quarter-mile times were within a few tenths of a second of the Super Bee and Charger.

Plymouth's Duster did not undergo any dramatic changes for 1971, merely improvement on a winning design. For the Duster 340, only the front grille and rear taillight designs were new, to distinguish it from the

This special blacked-out hood with bold graphics giving engine displacement was optional on 1971 Duster 340's.

'70 model. There was a new body side tape stripe with the number 340 featured prominently on the rear quarter panels. There was a total of eighteen exterior colors to choose from; twelve were new for 1971. The extra-cost colors, such as Tor-Red, Curious Yellow, In-Violet, Sassy Grass Green or Bahama Yellow, made the Duster 340 a standout. Inside, the standard plaid cloth-and-vinyl interior, color-keyed to the exterior, added excitement. The instrument panel in the Duster 340 featured large round dials, instead of warning lights, to give the driver all relevant engine functions instantly.

For 1971, Plymouth gave more specific performance specifications about the Duster 340. That year, Plymouth switched from a Carter AVS four-barrel carburetor to a Carter Thermo-Quad four-barrel carburetor on its high-performance 340 V-8. It was rated at 275 gross horsepower, with a net rating of 235 hp. The compression ratio was lowered an insignificant 0.2 to 10.3:1. Suspension specifications remained unchanged from 1970. Heavy-duty drum brakes, front and rear, were now standard and the front disc/rear drum brake arrangement was made optional.

To make your Duster even more significant on the street, the option list could accommodate you. New for '71 was a bold blacked-out hood paint treatment with stock-car-sized 340 on the hood outlined in white. Painted vertically inside the 4 was the word wedge in orange. With this hood treatment, there was no question what was underneath. You could add to the '71 Duster 340's base list price of $2,703 by ordering either the TorqueFlight automatic transmission or the heavy-duty four-speed manual transmission. Ordering either also meant spending more money for the front bucket seats and center console arrangement. With the four-speed manual transmission, you could really show you meant business by ordering the pistol-grip shift handle. In TorqueFlight automatic-transmission-equipped Duster 340's with the center console, a T-bar shift handle could be ordered. For the audio-minded, there was a new radio tape cassette with the ability to record off the radio, plus a microphone for dictation. For a racier look, you could order a rear spoiler. Although the Duster 340 had no optional engines, there were optional axle ratios to improve your times

The front bench seat in the 1971 Duster could be replaced with optional bucket seats.

A manually operated vinyl sun roof was a new option on 1971 Dusters. A welded steel frame around the opening reinforced the roof, giving it strength equivalent to an all-steel roof.

on the street or strip. The standard 3.23:1 rear axle could be switched for either a 3.55:1 or 3.91:1 ratio, both with Sure-Grip.

The Duster 340 was the top of the Valiant line for 1971. Just below it was a new model introduced at mid-year, called the Duster Twister. It provided performance "show," but without the "go." It may have been Plymouth's first image car—a car conveying a performance image without the hardware to back it up. Plymouth had a specific reason for this. The insurance industry began cracking down on performance cars in the early seventies by issuing alarmingly high premiums. Even the Duster 340 wasn't exempt, due to its considerable power-to-weight ratio, which was the formula insurance companies used to set premiums for performance cars. Plymouth responded by offering the Duster Twister.

The Twister was essentially a performance appearance package. Standard equipment included "dust swirl" side tape stripes, Duster 340 grille, a set of four Rallye road wheels less trim rings, dual racing mirrors, flat-black hood performance paint with strobe stripes, 6.95x14 white sidewall tires, plaid cloth-and-vinyl trim interior available in four colors, lower deck stripes and Twister decals on the rear quarter panels. Options included twin hood scoops, trim rings and bias-belted double-stripe white sidewall tires. Either the 198-ci six or the 318-ci V-8 was standard. The 225-ci six was the only optional engine. Plymouth described the Twister this way: "It's youth-oriented. It's low-priced. And it's insurable."

Having just made its debut in 1971, the Dodge Dart Demon did not exhibit many styling or mechanical changes for 1972. The front grille and rear taillights were slightly restyled. The Demon 340 continued, with the only significant change occurring to the engine. Compression ratio was now 8.5:1, down from 10.5:1. Despite this drop in compression and the adoption of net horsepower ratings, the high-performance 340 V-8 was now rated at 240 hp, a "loss" of only 35 hp. By comparison, the high-performance four-barrel 440 V-8, rated at 370 hp in 1971, dropped to 280 hp in 1972. The next-highest performance four-barrel 440 V-8 in 1972 was rated at 230 hp; the four-barrel 340 V-8 actually developed ten more horsepower than this 440 V-8 in 1972! The price of the 1972 Demon 340 rose only $38 from 1971—less than two percent.

The 1972 Plymouth Duster, like the Dodge Demon, also remained relatively unchanged. Plymouth introduced an electronic ignition system as standard which virtually eliminated ignition tuneups when low-lead fuel was used.

Inside, new thin-back front seats helped increase rear legroom. The standard Duster and Duster 340 cloth-and-vinyl split-back bench seat was available in blue, green, and black with white. There were three optional interiors for the Dusters. First, there were space-age-looking all-vinyl bucket seats available in black and white with black. Second, there was an all-vinyl split-back bench seat offered in blue, green, black and gold. Third, there was an all-vinyl bench seat with a folding center armrest in green, black, gold, and white with black.

The Duster's standard instrument panel continued using gauges instead of warning lights, and featured simulated wood graining. This dash was also used in the Valiant and the Scamp.

You could have your Duster in one of more than ten exterior colors, complemented with an optional vinyl roof in one of four colors.

The standard Duster engine was still a choice of either the one-barrel 198-ci slant six or the two-barrel 318-ci V-8. The Duster 340's engine had a rating of 240 net hp. The biggest engine you could get in a Plymouth Barracuda in 1972 was this four-barrel 340 V-8, so the 'Cuda had no performance advantage over the less-expensive Duster 340.

You could still get many performance-related options in your Duster or Duster 340, such as four-speed manual transmission, Hurst shifter with pistol grip, Sure-Grip differential, Rallye road wheels and Tuff steering wheel.

The list prices for the 1972 Duster and Duster 340 actually went down. That year the Duster sold for $2,287 and the Duster 340 sold for $2,742. In between these two cars was the Duster Twister, available again for 1972.

There were a number of changes to the Dodge Dart lineup for 1973. The Demon was no longer a model name. In its place were the Dart Sport and Dart Sport 340. Then came the Dart Swinger and Dart Swinger Special. Finally, there was the four-door Dart Custom. All Dart models had bigger, stronger bumpers designed to meet the new government-imposed bumper standards. Front end styling was also new; with the new front bumper, this gave the car a heavier look.

On the Dart Sport models, Dodge introduced two new options. A manual sliding metal sun roof gave the open-air sensation of a convertible. The other option, borrowed from the 1964 Barracuda, featured a fold-down rear seat and security panel, giving the owner station-wagon-like carrying capacity. Thus, the owner had either a two-door coupe, a convertible or a station wagon all in one car. Dodge coined a word for it: Convertriple.

Even when detuned for emissions, the 1973 high-performance 340 V-8 used in the Dart Sport 340 and Duster 340 still developed 240 net hp. This engine is shown with the air-conditioning compressor.

The Convertriple was the basis for a Dodge specialty show car, the *Hang 10,* displayed at the Chicago Auto Show for 1973 new model cars. This car was a styling study using a Dart Sport Convertriple to show how unusual materials, patterns, color combinations and graphics could give a car a personalized look keyed to locales, hobbies or interests.

The *Hang 10* was an example of such a car directed toward surfers. The car took its name from the surfing expression for balancing at the end of a surfboard with ten toes over the nose of the board while riding the wave. The fold-down security panel permitted loading the surfboard through the trunk. With no need to carry the surfboard on top, the sun roof could let the sunshine in. These two features were already available on the Dart Sport, but the *Hang 10* went further with the surfing theme.

Swimsuit material in various colored stripes was set into the seats and door panels. Brilliant orange carpet covered the back of the fold-down rear seat. The orange was picked up on the dash and the center console. The swimsuit material pattern was repeated in the exterior side stripe, with graphics on the rear quarter panels showing a surfer on a wave. Topping off the exterior theme was a surfboard design running down the center of the hood.

The *Hang 10* was an attempt by Dodge stylists to better determine consumer preferences in a declining performance market. Interviewers at the show questioned people at random to determine their reaction to the car.

In March of 1973, Dodge introduced a new Dart model in response to a market condition. That car was the Dart Sport Rallye. Robert D. Loomis was Dodge general sales manager at the time, and in a public relations press release, he explained the car's concept. "In an industry-wide shift of many buyers away from the muscle or specialty compact car, there has been a trend toward the smaller, less powerful car which is both economical and fun to drive. And the Dart Rallye is just such a car for men and women who enjoy driving."

The Dart Sport Rallye was aimed at a different kind of driver than the one primarily interested in thrilling acceleration. The key to the car's concept lay in its name. Road rallying is a form of competitive driving where acceleration is not an issue, but handling and braking are. It was with this

The *Hang 10* Dart Sport displayed at the Chicago Auto Show for 1973 cars used unique fabric, patterns, colors and a distinctive name to theme the car.

kind of driving in mind that Dodge adopted the name, and applied it to the Charger and Challenger models, as well.

The Dart Sport Rallye came equipped with the 150-hp two-barrel 318 V-8, four-speed close-ratio manual transmission, 3.23:1 rear axle ratio (a 3.55:1 axle was optional), front disc brakes, Rallye suspension, E70x14 raised white-letter tires, Rallye wheels, Tuff steering wheel and Dodge lettering on the rear quarter panels. A deluxe vinyl bench seat was standard, but bucket seats were optional.

Over in the Plymouth camp, the Duster had become Plymouth's best-selling model, largely due to the Duster's handsome styling. Consequently, Plymouth decided not to make any radical changes for 1973. The front end did receive some facelifting, primarily to incorporate the new extra-protection bumper system. The new grille and hood contributed to the car's somewhat heavy appearance.

In its 1973 brochure covering the Duster, performance was further deemphasized (the Rapid Transit System was no more) while "Extra care in engineering" was stressed. For 1973, the Duster had all the standard and optional features of the Dodge Dart, such as electronic ignition, sun roof and the fold-down rear seat and security panel which Plymouth called the Spacesaver Pak. When you ordered the optional sun roof, it became

In mid-1973, Dodge introduced the Dart Sport Rallye in response to an industry-wide trend away from muscle cars to less-powerful but still fun-to-drive cars. The 318 V-8 and four-speed manual transmission were standard.

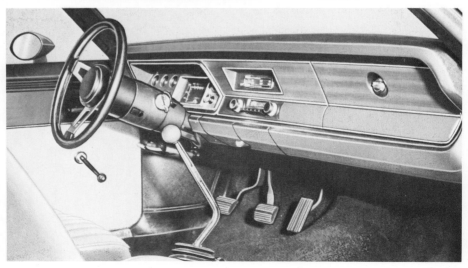

the Space Duster. There were no major changes with interior or exterior color offerings. The list price for the Duster went up nearly $100 to $2,376.

Despite the soft market for performance cars, Plymouth continued to advertise the Duster 340 in the enthusiast magazines. This ad copy proved Plymouth was still in there swinging: "Try to find a performance car that comes with heavy-duty torsion bars, heavy-duty rear springs, a front sway bar, high-control shocks, a dual exhaust system, 3.21:1 ratio rear axle, unibody construction and an engine equal to our 340-cubic-inch Wedge.

"Try to find a car like that for around $2800. Just try."

Plymouth was right. An equivalent car from Ford, Chevy or Pontiac cost hundreds of dollars more than the Duster 340. It was a lot of car—and fun—for the money. That 340 wedge V-8 still pumped out 240 net horsepower.

If you didn't want the Duster 340's performance but did want to draw looks, the Twister package was again offered. For 1973, the Twister package had a new blacked-out hood treatment and smaller nonfunctional hood scoops.

Chrysler bumped the displacement of its high-performance small-block V-8 from 340 to 360 ci for 1974. It was now rated at 245 hp. Torque went up nearly ten percent. Both the Plymouth Duster 360 and Dodge Dart Sport 360 got this engine.

In 1974, the Dodge Dart Sport 360 with the new 360-ci V-8 was introduced. The Plymouth Duster 360 got the same powerplant.

Plymouth in particular talked about the high-performance 360 V-8's heritage. "Our 360 high-performance engine should be especially appealing to any buffs in the crowd," the brochure read. "It has many of the same time-tested components found in its famous predecessor—the 340. Its features include a four-barrel carburetor, shot-peened crankshaft, heavy-duty bearings, high performance camshaft, special intake and exhaust valves (the stems of the exhaust valves are chrome plated for improved scuff resistance), high load valve springs with surge dampers, double roller timing chain, oil pan windage tray, slip drive fan and dual exhausts."

However, both the high-performance Dart and Duster gained nearly 150 pounds over 1971 models in response to the bumper standards and Chrysler-imposed soundproofing. The added weight and decreased overall performance from three years before affected acceleration. While test results can sometimes vary wildly, 0-60 mph and quarter-mile times increased roughly two seconds compared to those for the 1970 Duster.

The Duster 360 took a startling price jump over the Duster 340. Plymouth's high-performance compact now cost $3,212—nearly $400 more

The Plymouth Duster and Valiant were the sturdy cars used by Dan Fleenor's Hurricane Hell Drivers in the early seventies.

than the year before. The Dart Sport 360 experienced an identical price increase.

Aside from the engine, there wasn't much new offered in either model that year. Plymouth and Dodge still made available such performance options as the four-speed manual transmission, Hurst shifter and Sure-Grip differential with 3.55:1 axle ratio; but buyers weren't going for performance as they had in the late sixties and early seventies. The sportier cars in the Dodge and Plymouth lines—the Challenger and Barracuda—were phased out in 1974 and the Dart Sport and Duster eventually joined them at the end of the 1976 model year.

CHAPTER TWELVE

The Last Charge(r)
1971-1974

*T*he Dodge Charger was completely restyled for 1971. While it did not have the "machined steel" look of the second generation, it retained enough of the styling to bear a resemblance. Dodge had not recouped the cost of modifying the production Charger 500 and Daytona rear windows, so the third-generation Charger featured a semifastback roofline with flush rear window, and an integral rear deck spoiler more pronounced than on the previous Charger.

There were numerous changes or improvements on the '71 Charger. Wheelbase was shortened from 117 inches to 115 inches. The windshield wipers were now concealed, with an articulated blade on the driver's side. Outside door handles were flush. The windows were now ventless. In one of its first steps toward government-mandated pollution control, Dodge featured the Vapor Saver, which prevented much of the gas tank evaporation from escaping.

There were six distinct Charger models for 1971. The Charger coupe was the lowest-priced model at $2,707. This was a dramatic price reduction of nearly $300 from the 1970 base list price, achieved by the use of less-expensive, fixed rear quarter windows and exposed headlights. Standard engines were either the 225-ci six-cylinder or the 318-ci V-8.

Next up the Charger ladder was, simply, the Charger hardtop. Included or changed were: color-keyed carpeting, cigarette lighter, simulated wood-grain door trim inserts and instrument panel appliqué, color-keyed steering wheel with simulated wood-grain insert and inside day/night mirror. The same standard engines were offered.

The Charger 500 was again available, but it was not a high-performance model. The only essential difference between the Charger and the Charger 500 was the use of bucket seats with integral head restraints in the latter. Other niceties were included with the 500, however: hooded, circular instrumentation with all gauges, as in previous high-performance Chargers; glovebox light; map/courtesy light; ashtray light; side paint stripes; and deluxe wheelcovers. The standard engine was the 318 V-8. Base list price was $3,973.

For an extra $200, you could order the Charger SE. This was the only Charger model in 1971 with concealed headlights standard; they were optional on other models. The SE also had a different grille. It had all the amenities of the Charger 500, as well as an ignition switch light with time delay, instrument panel hood release, split-back cloth-and-vinyl bench seat with center armrest, carpeted trunk and landau vinyl roof in four available colors. The Charger SE didn't hold much interest for the Mopar enthusiast, but the next two models did.

New for 1971 was the Charger Super Bee. The Coronet Super Bee had been Dodge's answer to Plymouth's Road Runner for a low-buck, high-performance street machine; for 1971 this concept was switched to the Charger. This new member of the Dodge Scat Pack was powered by a 300-hp 383-ci four-barrel Magnum V-8 with a compression ratio lowered to 8.7 to run on regular fuel. The transmission was a three-on-the-floor manual. Despite its economy label, it had the same interior appointments as the Charger 500, except for the full-width front bench seat used in the Super Bee.

This photo shows several options offered in the 1971 Charger, including a Tuff 14½-inch steering wheel, Hurst shifter with pistol grip, and cassette recorder and playback machine.

The 1971 Charger R/T was distinguished from the Super Bee by R/T medallions and two fake vents on the doors.

Outside, the Charger Super Bee had a prominent power bulge on the hood, and—for the first time on a Charger—a functional Ramcharger hood scoop that popped up when the accelerator was floored. The power bulge was blacked-out, and brandished a Super Bee decal. A black longitudinal performance tape stripe ran from the cowl at the base of the windshield, as part of the blacked-out hood treatment, then along the sides of the car to the rear fender cap. Color-keyed bumpers could be ordered, and these made the Super Bee look even more purposeful.

Underneath, the Super Bee benefited from a Rallye Suspension Package, which included heavy-duty torsion bars and rear springs, front anti-

1971 was the first and only year that the Charger was available with the Ramcharger fresh-air hood scoop. It was optional on the Charger Super Bee and standard on the Charger R/T.

The Dodge Charger Super Bee was a new model for 1971. This one is shown with optional Ramcharger hood scoop and color-keyed bumpers.

163

sway bar, heavy-duty shocks and heavy-duty drum brakes that measured 11x3 inches up front and 11x2½ inches at the rear. F70x14 wide-tread tires were standard. The Charger Super Bee was priced at $4,043.

If you wanted more "umph," you could order the 440 Six-Pack or 426 Hemi. You were wise if you also ordered the Super Trak Pak Performance Axle Package with the limited-slip Dana 4.10 rear end to handle the torque, and a manual four-speed with pistol-grip Hurst shifter, dual-breaker distributor, a bigger radiator and a seven-blade fan. This package was conceived with drag racing in mind. If you drove your Super Bee primarily on the street, the Trak Pak was sufficient. It had all the heavy-duty parts of the Super Trak Pak, but with a more reasonable 3.54 rear end ratio.

At the top of the Charger line was the R/T, with a list price of $4,311. As always, it was powered by the venerable four-barrel 440 Magnum V-8. This engine ran a 9.7:1 compression ratio requiring premium fuel and pumped out 370 gross hp. It was coupled to Chrysler's superb TorqueFlight automatic with the gear selector on the steering column. The 425-hp 426 Hemi and the 385-hp 440 Six-Pack (down five horsepower from 1970) were optional. The R/T's interior differed from the Super Bee's only in the use of front bucket seats.

The 1971 Charger 500 was a luxury car, not a limited-production high-performance car as in 1969.

The 1971 Charger SE was the only Charger model that year with standard concealed headlights.

As in previous years, the R/T's suspension components were extra-heavy-duty, using high-rate torsion bars, heavy-duty shocks, extra-heavy-duty rear springs with special right rear spring and front antisway bar. This same suspension was included in the engine package for Hemi- and 440 Six-Pack-equipped Chargers.

Externally, the R/T had the same blacked-out hood bulge and longitudinal tape stripe as the Super Bee. It was identifiable by the R/T logo on the hood and rear trunk lid, and R/T medallions on the front fenders. Also, the R/T had two curved tape stripes on the doors, simulating vents.

New on the option list and of interest to Mopar enthusiasts were front and rear spoilers. The rear spoiler was similar in design and function to that used on the 1969 Pontiac GTO Judge. Few buyers chose to order their Chargers with these spoilers, however.

A two-barrel version of the 400-ci V-8, equipped with a Holley carburetor, was optional in 1972 Chargers.

The Charger Rallye was the only performance model in 1972; the Charger Super Bee and R/T were no longer offered. A 280-hp four-barrel 440 V-8 was the strongest powerplant available in the car. Note the simulated door vents.

There were three paint and stripe options besides the standard one. First was the standard blacked-out hood, with the longitudinal stripe deleted. Next was the blacked-out hood with longitudinal stripe running up and over the optional rear spoiler. The third choice was the blacked-out hood (no longitudinal stripe) with a broad bumblebee stripe. This last combination was available in red, black, white, blue or green.

Charger buyers were not disappointed with their car's performance that year. A Super Bee with optional 440 Six-Pack could reach 60 mph in 6.9 seconds and do the quarter mile in 14.0 seconds. A Hemi-equipped Super Bee, weighing almost 100 pounds more, reached 60 mph in an astounding 5.7 seconds and the quarter mile in only 13.7 seconds.

This set the high-water mark for Dodge Charger performance. Never again would Mopar enthusiasts enjoy the freedom of choice and levels of performance established in 1971.

Charger buyers looking for muscle in 1972 found their options reduced considerably. The R/T and Super Bee models were dropped. The only performance model was the Charger Rallye, available as a coupe or hardtop.

The Rallye retained the performance hood bulge with blacked-out treatment, but the Ramcharger pop-up scoop was gone. Included in the Rallye package was a sculptured dark grille, simulated door louvers with blacked-out treatment, and louvered black taillights. The Rallye suspension was a bit softer than the R/T suspension, but included front and rear anti-sway bars. The car rode on F70x14 wide-tread, white sidewall tires. The interior featured a new split-back front bench seat. The rest of the interior remained essentially unchanged.

Drastic changes took place in the Rallye's engine compartment. The 426 Hemi was dropped. The 440 Six-Pack was offered—it was listed as an optional engine in the 1972 Charger brochure—but was also dropped before initial production. The remaining engines were redesigned to meet emissions standards, not performance standards. The 318 V-8 was standard in the Rallye. The first optional engine was the 340 4-bbl. All Chrysler engines had lowered compression ratios to run on unleaded gas; the 340 V-8 had a compression ratio of 8.2:1. Chrysler also adopted net horsepower

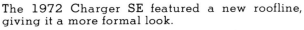

The 1972 Charger SE featured a new roofline,
giving it a more formal look.

ratings; the 340 V-8 was rated at 240. The 383 V-8 was replaced by a new 400, offered in a 2-bbl and two 4-bbl versions. The 400 4-bbl V-8 was rated at 255 hp. The top engine was the 280-hp 440 4-bbl V-8; the TorqueFlight was standard with this engine.

The standard 2.94:1 rear axle ratio for V-8-equipped Chargers could be improved upon. There was a Performance Axle Package (not available with three-speed manual transmission or 400-ci 2-bbl V-8). A Trak Pak package, with a 3.55:1 Sure-Grip rear axle, was available only with the 440 V-8 and four-speed manual transmission. The Sure-Grip differential was still offered separately.

Despite the reduced number of choices for 1972, one could still put together a high-performance Charger if the options were chosen carefully. The Charger Rallye with 440 4-bbl V-8, four-speed manual transmission and Trak Pak had respectable performance.

In 1973, the Charger received some subtle facelifting. The front grille and rear taillights were new. The SE no longer had concealed headlights. The rear roofline was also new, with the roof pillars angled forward instead of back. Performance was deemphasized, with new stress on making the Charger a quieter, more comfortable, personal luxury car.

The Charger Rallye Package was again available on the coupe and hardtop. The changes were primarily cosmetic. The blacked-out treatment on the hood was slightly different to permit the car's body color to show through on the sides of the power bulge, with the word Rallye in black. Hood tie-down pins were part of the package for the first time on the Charger. They were standard on the Rallye and optional on other models.

The body shell of the 1974 Charger remained unchanged after four years. The Charger's performance and image *had* changed dramatically, however.

A gradated body side tape stripe in black or red accented the Charger's curving contours. Raised white-letter F70x14 tires were now standard.

Underneath, the Charger's suspension was softened considerably, and this altered the car's brisk handling abilities. The extra-heavy-duty suspension for the 440 V-8 Charger was history.

The 440 4-bbl V-8 was still available, though. It was now rated at 280 net horsepower. The Charger was starting to feel the effects of ever-increasing emissions controls. A Charger SE with the 440 V-8 could reach 60 mph in 7.4 seconds, but the quarter mile took over fifteen seconds to cover, due primarily to its 4,160-pound curb weight.

Power made a slight drop in 1974. The 440 4-bbl V-8 now had 275 net hp. Enthusiasts had to look to other manufacturers' cars if they wanted more horsepower under the hood.

Actually, Dodge was only responding to market trends, and government regulations. Although a fair number of 1974 Chargers were Rallyes, the majority of Chargers were purchased as personal luxury cars. The demise of the full-size performance car was long in coming. Dodge kept the performance image of its Charger alive longer than necessary, perhaps— but by 1975, when the Charger was completely redesigned, the transition to luxury car status was complete.

The 1974 Charger SE featured a new roof treatment with louvered side windows. The sun roof was optional.

CHAPTER THIRTEEN

Direct Connection: The Mighty Mopar Legacy

"*T*hey once roamed the face of the North American continent in great numbers. They were awesome, powerful beasts, shaking the earth beneath them. While they existed, they were feared by the weak. Their stay on this planet was brief—less than two decades. They are gone now—extinct. A few remain, like massive metal dinosaurs. They were the Mighty Mopars, and we will never see their like again."

This could be the epitaph of Dodge and Plymouth performance cars, if ever a tombstone were to be erected. During the muscle car era, enthusiasts never thought that it might end. Each new year brought ever more powerful engines and ever faster cars. In the euphoria brought on by almost frightening acceleration coupled with the gutteral roar of the engine, the likelihood of such performance disappearing completely seemed impossible.

Indeed, it never entered our minds. However, by the mid-seventies, it was clear that performance was all but absent. In hindsight, the muscle car era came and went too quickly. Many enthusiasts wish they could turn the clock back, yearning for the days when they could walk into a Dodge or Plymouth showroom and order a Hemi 'Cuda or Six-Pack Road Runner. And find good, cheap gas to put in it.

In the early seventies, Chrysler saw that the end was near. Having supported racers and street enthusiasts for so many years, it felt it should continue to do so, even if Chrysler—like other car manufacturers—was no longer in the high-performance production car business. In fact, Chrysler had already laid the groundwork during the muscle car heyday.

Dick Maxwell explained how this came about. "We built our race cars —production performance cars—on the assembly line. [They] were sold like regular production cars, and they were serviced as such. Now, the mortality rate among these cars that were raced was much higher than our production cars, so there were never any parts. So we—the race group— laid out our own supply of parts. We had our own inventory of blocks, cranks, pistons, heads, transmissions and so forth. We serviced the guys we were supporting out of that. The other racers out there who were not factory sponsored came crying to us for parts because they couldn't get them out of the parts division; they were always back ordered.

"So," Maxwell continued, "we began selling parts direct to customers. We'd ship parts COD or the guy would mail us a check and we'd send him a crankshaft or whatever, simply to keep these guys going. All the time, we were telling the parts division to stock and sell the parts. This went on for a while. Finally, the parts division put together their Hustle Stuff program in 1969."

The Hustle Stuff catalog listed high-performance parts for all Chrysler V-8's, from the 273 to the 426 Hemi and 440. Also listed were modifications to existing engines. This gave the Mopar enthusiast the information he needed to make his car a competitor at the drag strip while maintaining streetability. Parts were also listed for suspensions, rear ends, even gauges. In the back of the catalog were listed performance parts packages, which combined a number of appearance or performance parts, saving the buyer frustration and money.

"The Hustle Stuff program ran well for a while," Maxwell said, "but finally folded. Then, the race group finally got corporate approval to go into the parts business outside of the Chrysler parts division about 1971. We had our own warehouse, but distributed through dealers. That's really how the Direct Connection program came to be. Joe Schulte, working on his own, came up with the Direct Connection name and put together the early advertising while moonlighting at home."

In an effort to expand its high-performance parts availability, corporate approval was again granted in the mid-seventies to sell Direct Connection parts through speed shops. Despite the decline of performance in the showroom, enthusiasm for keeping mighty Mopars on the streets and strips continued to grow, thanks to the Direct Connection program.

Historically, Dodge and Plymouth divisions never merely sold high-performance cars and parts; they offered advice as well. This advice, in the form of bulletins, was compiled and makes up the *Direct Connection Performance Book.* Known as the Big Book at Chrysler, it rivals the Manhattan phone book in thickness. These bulletins came from Chrysler staff engineers with many years of experience and enthusiasm for Mopar performance cars. Staff engineer Larry Shepard is the principle coordinator of the Direct Connection Development program.

The parts are listed in the Direct Connection catalogs. The Direct Connection program is based on supplying high-performance parts for Mopar V-8 engines from the sixties and seventies as well as parts for Chrysler's 2.2-liter four-cylinder engine of the eighties. Some parts for the big-block V-8's, such as crankshafts, are no longer offered because they are no longer manufactured by Chrysler. However, guidelines and recommendations on how to rebuild the big V-8's and modify the existing 2.2-liter engine for maximum performance are in one catalog. Another catalog lists parts for chassis.

Engine and chassis modification books published by Chrysler Corporation for its Direct Connection program.

In the mid-seventies, Chrysler instituted a research and development program to come up with parts for the high-performance 340 V-8. The W-2 cylinder heads and induction system, among other parts, were results of that program. Although even the 340 and 360 V-8's are no longer built for use in cars, millions of small- and big-block Chrysler engines in junkyards and on the streets provide bracket racers an almost unlimited supply of hardware. Chrysler recommends the best engine to build from is one with many hot and cold cycles, so the block is thoroughly "cured" or "seasoned." With so many such engines available, there really is no need to manufacture fresh blocks, with some exceptions.

The bulk of engine research and development in the eighties is on the 2.2-liter engine. The Direct Connection catalog of today reflects this. Despite the reduction in engine size, Chrysler is enthused about developing this engine and related Direct Connection parts to build a powerplant with a horsepower-per-cubic-inch ratio to match that of its old big-block V-8's. Closely tied with this is the improvement of vehicle power-to-weight ratio, aerodynamics, handling and fuel economy.

For mighty Mopar enthusiasts, it is gratifying to know many of the key people at Chrysler during the super car sixties are still there—and they are still excited by performance. The Direct Connection program promises to keep performance alive in the hearts and minds of hundreds of thousands of Dodge and Plymouth performance car owners.

The Direct Connection books are packed with technical information and helpful advice.

INDEX

MORE GREAT READING

American Car Spotter's Guide 1940-1965. Covers 66 makes—almost 3,000 illustrations. 358 pages, softbound.

American Car Spotter's Guide 1966-1980. Giant pictorial source with over 3,600 illustrations. 432 pages, softbound.

The Production Figure Book For U.S. Cars. Reflects the relative rarity of various makes, models, body styles, etc. Softbound, 180 pages.

Pontiac: The Postwar Years. One of America's most exciting makes of automobile is described in this factual 33-year history. 256 photos, 205 pages.

Chevy Super Sports 1961-1976. Exciting story of these hot cars with complete specs and data. 176 pages, 234 illustrations, softbound. Large format.

Son of Muscle Car Mania. 176 pages of more great ads from the 1962-1974 muscle car era. All U.S. makes represented. Softbound, 250 illustrations.

Muscle Car Mania. A collection of advertisements for muscle cars 1964 through 1974. 176 pages, 250 illustrations, softbound.

Fearsome Fords 1959-1973. Over 250 photos of these great cars accompany 182 pages of interesting information. Softbound, large format.

Auto Restoration From Junker to Jewel. Illustrated guide to restoring old cars. 292 pages, 289 illustrations, softbound.

Corvair Affair. The whole Corvair story including styling, mechanicals and the Nader connection. 176 pages, over 140 great illustrations.

Shelby's Wildlife: The Cobras and Mustangs. Complete, exciting story of the 260, 289, 427 and Daytona Cobras plus Shelby Mustangs. 224 pages, nearly 200 photos.

Classic Motorbooks Ford Retractable 1957-1959 Photofacts. Nearly 200 photos help tell this unique story. Softbound, 80 pages.

Illustrated Porsche Buyer's Guide. Covers the 356 through the 944 from 1950 to 1983 with lots of photos. Softbound, 175 pages.

Porsches For The Road. Beautiful photo essays on 12 models. In the Survivors Series. 128 pages, 250 illustrations, 125 in color.

The Big "Little GTO" Book. All of these Great Ones by Pontiac are covered—1965-1974. Over 150 great photos, 235 pages. Large format, softbound.

How To Restore Your Collector Car. Covers all the major restoration processes in an easy-to-understand, easy-to-use format. More than 300 illustrations. Softbound, 320 pages.

Harley-Davidson Motor Company: An Official Eighty-Year History. More than 250 photos plus 8 pages of color tell the complete story 1903-1983. 288 pages.

Classic Motorbooks Chevy El Camino 1959-1982 Photofacts. 80 pages packed full of info on these car/trucks. Softbound, about 200 photos.

Classic Motorbooks Chrysler 300 1955-1961 Photofacts. Over 125 photos accompany lots of info on these cars. Softbound, 80 pages.

Classic Motorbooks Pontiac Trans Am 1969-1973 Photofacts. Over 125 great photos help tell the story. 80 pages, softbound.

Bob Bondurant on High Performance Driving. World-famous instructor teaches secrets to fast, safe driving. Over 100 illustrations, 144 pages, softbound.

Panteras For The Road. Over 250 illustrations, many in color cover these great cars, 125 pages. In the Survivors Series.

Automotive Fuel Injection Systems: A Technical Guide. Thorough analysis and description of current gas-engine technology. 173 illustrations, 182 pages, softbound.

The Art and Science of Grand Prix Driving. Complete analysis and discussion by World Champion Niki Lauda. Over 150 photos, 23 in color, 245 pages.

Autocourse. Large-format racing annual. Coverage of each Grand Prix and other major racing events and series. Over 200 pages with lots of color.

Illustrated High Performance Mustang Buyer's Guide. Covers the 1965 GT, the Shelby, through the 1973 Mach 1. Softbound, 250 illustrations, 176 pages.

Illustrated Alfa Romeo Buyer's Guide. The 6C-2500 through the Montreal are covered with over 200 illustrations. 176 pages, softbound.

Illustrated Ferrari Buyer's Guide. Features all street/production cars 1954 through 1980. 176 pages, over 225 photos, softbound.

Illustrated Corvette Buyer's Guide. Includes 194 photos and lots of info on all these cars 1953-1982. 156 pages, softbound.

Illustrated M.G. Buyer's Guide. Features all the models 1924 through 1982. 160 pages, softbound, over 125 illustrations.

Illustrated Lamborghini Buyer's Guide. Details all models from the first V-12-engined 350 GTV through the 1983 LMA models including many specials. 176 pages, over 250 photos, softbound.

Motorbooks International®
Publishers & Wholesalers Inc.
Osceola, Wisconsin 54020, USA